SCIENCE, MATH, CHECKMATE

32 Chess Activities for Inquiry and Problem Solving

Alexey W. Root

Foreword by Dr. Max and Hiroko Warshauer

Teacher **Ideas** Press

An imprint of Libraries Unlimited
Westport, Connecticut • London

Library of Congress Cataloging-in-Publication Data

Root, Alexey W.
  Science, math, checkmate : 32 chess activities for inquiry and problem solving
/ Alexey W. Root ; foreword by Max and Hiroko Warshauer.
     p. cm.
  Includes bibliographical references and index.
  ISBN 978–1–59158–571–8 (alk. paper)
  1. Chess—End games.   I. Title.
  GV1450.7.R55 2008
  794.1'24—dc22   2007040758

British Library Cataloguing in Publication Data is available.

Library of Congress Catalog Card Number: 2007040758
ISBN: 978–1–59158–571–8

First published in 2008

Libraries Unlimited/Teacher Ideas Press, 88 Post Road West, Westport, CT 06881
A Member of the Greenwood Publishing Group, Inc.
www.lu.com

Printed in the United States of America

The paper used in this book complies with the
Permanent Paper Standard issued by the National
Information Standards Organization (Z39.48–1984).

10 9 8 7 6 5 4 3 2 1

For Kornelijs (Neil) Dale,
respected tournament director,
valued friend

CONTENTS

Chapter 3 Mathematical Problem Solving   37

 Chapter 4 Interdisciplinary   65

FOREWORD

Science, Math, Checkmate is the second book by educator and chess expert Dr. Alexey Root that deftly weaves chess into the educational fabric of school mathematics and science. As in her first book, *Children and Chess: A Guide for Educators,* this book is a rich resource of activities educators can use to engage, enrich, and enhance student learning.

Teaching problem solving is one of the most challenging tasks for mathematics and science teachers. Chess provides an intriguing context for students to explore a variety of intellectually demanding problems while encouraging students to explain and justify their solutions. The 32 activities found in this book are designed to encourage students to experiment with strategies, visualize relationships of pieces, and reason through their moves and consequences.

Written as a resource book for teachers that links to national mathematics and science standards, each activity includes Objectives, Materials, and Procedures, and is designed to take the students 30 to 45 minutes to complete. In addition, the activities are notated with grade appropriateness that ranges from grades 3 to 8 and sequenced according to the extent of students' chess knowledge that is required. A chess test is included to gauge the chess knowledge of students. The author shares with us numerous activities that were inspired by her children, which suggest a very student-focused approach to the activities.

It is through our children that we first met Dr. Root. Over 15 years ago, Dr. Root offered chess lessons to children in Austin, Texas. Three of our four children were able to take lessons with Alexey, as they fondly called her, who instilled in them a great love for the game. As a mathematician and a mathematics educator we were fortunate to have Alexey write an article on chess and mathematics in *Math Reader* magazine, which was published by Texas Mathworks at Texas State University–San Marcos. We have been impressed by how she has used chess as a platform for teaching students to think creatively about problems while making learning fun and engaging. Teachers will find these activities to be a wonderful resource that they can use in their classrooms to stimulate excitement and curiosity about problem solving. At the same time, students will develop a foundation in chess that can be a lifelong source of fun and enjoyment that can be shared between people of all ages.

Max and Hiroko Warshauer
Department of Mathematics Texas State University–San Marcos

Chapter 1

THE CURRICULUM GAME

Curriculum Moves

"Curriculum is like a board game" (McNeil, 2006, p. 111; Purves, 1975). This simile resonated with me because of my affection for the board game of **chess.** Throughout *Science, Math, Checkmate,* chess terms are in **boldface** when they first appear; a glossary of those terms is located at the end of the book. My first curriculum **moves** included considering the role of chess in education; consulting national standards in science and math; rethinking my chess lesson plans; reviewing the work of other chess authors; and asking for ideas from my students, friends, family, and colleagues. After these **opening** moves, I wrote 32 activities—the **middlegame** of my curriculum. Each activity is 30–45 minutes long, features chess instruction, and teaches science and math. An answer key for the 32 activities is located in Appendix B. Throughout this book, and in summary form in chapter 5, I present the rules, **algebraic notation,** and basic concepts of chess.

Appendix A consists of a chess test and its answer key. Because the test contains examples of the chess concepts taught in this book, it may serve as pre-test, post-test, or both. Since the same chess concepts are taught to students in grades 3 through 5 and 6 through 8, use the test with both groups. In contrast, science and math objectives differ among grade levels. References—for which science and math goals are addressed by each activity and for sources used—are found after the glossary and before the index. Appendix C is a review of the curricula offered by the Kasparov and Polgar Chess Foundations.

The **endgame** was teaching my activities to students. Each time I taught, I reflected on what went well and what needed to be improved. My reflections caused me to revise activities. As you try these activities with your students, you may decide that further revisions are in order.

The Role of Chess

As shown in Figure 1.1, the decision process in chess "characterizes most complex, goal-directed thought and choice processes, scientific activity included" (Gobet, 1999, p. 89). Yet chess does not depend on academic subject-matter knowledge. Thus, for classrooms that have learners with varying levels of subject-matter expertise and English-language competence, chess enables the practice of inquiry and **heuristics.**

Gobet **Chess/Science** (1999, p. 89)	**Polya** **Mathematics** (1957, pp. xvi–xvii)
Orientation	Understanding the problem
Exploration	Devising a plan
Investigation	Carrying out the plan
Proof	Looking back

Figure 1.1.
Problem solving in science, chess, and math.

National Standards

Science

The chess activities in this book serve as a supplement to, not as a replacement for, science and math content. Science requires study of the natural world. Nevertheless, the critical-thinking processes of scientific inquiry may be practiced with chess activities. "Some [science] activities provide a basis for observation, data collection, reflection, and analysis of firsthand events and phenomena" (National Research Council, 1996, p. 33). Similarly, during chess games, students record moves. They analyze **wins, losses,** and **draws.** For the activities in chapter 2, students consider: What are the characteristics of chess **pieces** and **pawns?** What is the purpose of a science or chess model? By asking and answering questions such as these, students see themselves as inquirers.

Math

Chess is an authentic context for students' mathematical problem solving. The National Council of Teachers of Mathematics (NCTM) defined best practice:

Instructional programs from prekindergarten through grade 12 should enable all students to—build new mathematical knowledge through problem solving; solve problems that arise in mathematics and in other contexts; apply and adapt a variety of appropriate strategies to solve problems; [and] monitor and reflect on the process of mathematical problem solving. (2000, p. 52)

As shown in Figure 1.1, the chess and science heuristics correspond to those of mathematics. Some strategies recommended by Polya and NCTM for solving problems are "using diagrams, looking for patterns, listing all possibilities, trying special values or cases, working backward, guessing and checking, creating an equivalent problem, and creating a simpler problem" (NCTM, 2000, p. 54). The activities in chapter 3 incorporate many of these strategies. By figuring out solutions to math questions and chess **position**s, students see themselves as problem solvers.

Interdisciplinary

Chapter 4 draws from the wealth of material about chess, a game with "more than 1,500 years of continuous history . . . integrated into the creative and professional lives of artists, linguists, psychologists, economists, mathematicians, politicians, theologians, computer scientists, and generals" (Shenk, 2006, p. 4). The chess pawns and pieces serve as metaphors for historical, literary, and social concepts. For example, the names of the pieces and pawns reflect the social structure of Europe in the middle ages. The activities in chapter 4 connect chess literature and history with science and math.

Ideas and Inspiration

After drawing ideas from the national standards for science and math, I consulted students, friends, colleagues, my family, and other authors. Four of the activities were originally homework assignments from students in the **Chess in Education Certificate online courses.** Two of the activities came from **United States Chess Federation (USCF) masters.** Both played for the University of Texas at Dallas (UTD) chess team, http://chess.utdallas.edu/, and are experienced chess teachers. My husband Doug, an associate professor of biology at the University of North Texas and an **International Master** according to the **Fédération Internationale des Échecs (FIDE),** gave me the scientific background for concepts such as the black box.

Some of the activities have been a part of my curriculum—at chess camps, recreation center chess classes, private chess lessons, in-school chess classes, and after-school chess clubs—for many years. Several of those reused activities, such as the *Pawn Game* in chapter 2, are also well known in the chess instructional literature. In other cases, such as the **Pandolfini**-derived *Chess Models* activity in chapter 2, the work of other authors inspired me to write new activities. For ideas in this book that are part of the greater body of chess knowledge, I cited sources within activities and again in References. Those chess sources provide additional background for educators, such as more examples to use with students. My reasons for choosing these particular chess resources were:

1. the accuracy of the chess information;
2. the prestige of the author (chess title or years of experience as a chess teacher);
3. the availability of the source;
4. the cost of the source, with free sources given priority;
5. my familiarity with the source and its fit with my themes for this book; and
6. the date of publication. I favored chess instructional literature published within the last 15 years. When I chose older sources, they are reasonably priced classics.

White to move and checkmate in 1.

Caution: f8 (Q) is stalemate.

Figure 1.2.
Chess position created by a 10-year-old.

Many wonderful chess books have not been listed in References, for one or more of the reasons listed.

Some great ideas came from my children. I asked my son William to create a chess position where the **promotion** of a pawn to a **queen** would be a **stalemate,** but an **under-promotion** to a **knight** would be a **checkmate.** William had a USCF **rating** of 600, which is average for a 10-year-old **tournament** competitor. In three minutes William invented the position in Figure 1.2, which I then included in my online courses. The solution, in algebraic notation, is 1. f8(N)#, that is, pawn moves to f8, under-promotes to a knight (N), and white announces checkmate (#). For *Criteria Challenge* in chapter 2, I selected similar tasks from Pelts and Alburt (1992, pp. 75–124).

My 14-year-old daughter, Clarissa, thought of the key idea for chapter 4's *Move Order Mystery:* Students organize moves from a cut-up **score sheet** in a logical order, reminiscent of tasks where out-of-order sentences are reorganized in a paragraph. Clarissa's idea also had a science connection. Based on their knowledge of chess openings, students arrange the moves. They test their hypothesized move order using pawns and pieces. Clarissa also took both photos of me used in this book. I took the rest of the book's photos.

Having completed the opening moves of my *Science, Math, Checkmate* curriculum, I began the middlegame of typing. My pet rabbit Abba made writing time fun. For Root (2006) and for this present endeavor, I've petted Abba by reaching down from my computer chair as shown in Figure 1.3. I pet him every five sentences or so. These pauses to pet allow me to either reread my writing or to decide on my next paragraph. Sometimes we spend more than eight hours a day in (me) and under (Abba) the computer chair. My advice to writers needing an extra incentive to sit still and write: Adopt a rabbit, http://www.rabbit.org/.

Figure 1.3.
Abba with the author.

The endgame of *Science, Math, Checkmate* was administering the chess test and teaching the 32 activities. I have volunteered as a Denton Independent School District (D.I.S.D) chess teacher since 1999, the same year I began working at UTD. Dr. George Fair, Dean of General Studies at UTD, and the UTD Chess Program (Founder Dr. Tim Redman, Director James Stallings, Assistant Director Luis Salinas, and Coach Rade Milovanovic) have encouraged and supported my chess volunteering. That volunteering was instrumental in the development of materials for my first book (Root, 2006) and for this present endeavor.

Science, Math, Checkmate activities had trial runs in D.I.S.D. in December of 2006. Development continued throughout the spring semester (2007) of **chess club**s. At Evers Elementary, my son's fifth-grade teacher, Mrs. Tracy Hahnle, permitted me to test an activity with her 20 students. Mrs. Sondra Wilkerson, Evers EXPO (gifted-and-talented) teacher, organized a Friday recess-time (2:05–2:45) chess club for me to teach. In its first nine-week session, I paired 10 fifth-grade students with 10 students from Mr. Fermin Hernandez's bilingual third-grade classroom. The second nine-week session consisted of 14 third- and fourth-graders.

Mrs. Jackie Thompson, EXPO teacher at Strickland Middle School, allowed me to run a chess club in her room during each Friday's (1:10–1:55) advisory period in the spring semester. The club was open to all students in grades 6–8. Principals Tricia Bolz (Evers) and Mike Vance (Strickland), and librarians Judy Giese (Evers) and Rosemary Grose (Strickland), provided the following support: publicizing the chess clubs to students, providing space for chess tournaments, facilitating field trips, assisting with media coverage, and purchasing chess instructional books, software, trophies, and equipment.

By the time D.I.S.D. dismissed for summer break in late May 2007, the curriculum (still in manuscript form) functioned well. After input from my editor, Sharon Coatney, I revised further. I then used the Chess Test and activities in *Science, Math, Checkmate* with my summer chess campers in Coppell, TX, and Spring, TX. In June of 2007 I taught for two weeks at the M.O.S.A.I.C. (Marvelous Opportunities Scheduled as Individual Courses) summer enrichment organized by the Coppell Gifted Association http://www.coppellgifted.org. My M.O.S.A.I.C. chess courses, which ran from 9 A.M. to noon Monday through Friday, enrolled

14 students (week one) and 18 students (week two). My students were entering grades 4 through 8 in the upcoming fall, that is, "rising fourth through eighth graders." Students did not have to be in gifted programs, or be resident in Coppell I.S.D., to attend M.O.S.A.I.C. courses. Many students came to the M.O.S.A.I.C. chess courses with no prior knowledge of chess.

From July 9–13, I taught at the Klein Chess Camp in Spring, TX, directed by Jim Liptrap (see http://jliptrap.us/). My classes ran from Monday through Thursday and ranged from rising first graders through rising seventh graders. I had 9–12 students in each 50-minute class. Though all but a handful of my students knew how the pawns and pieces moved, instruction on (or review of) **en passant, castling,** algebraic notation, and stalemate was necessary. The fifth day of camp (Friday) was a chess tournament.

On August 2, at the invitation of my former online student and third-grade teacher Jody Braswell, I presented four of the *Science, Math, Checkmate* activities to 32 Ector Country I.S.D. K–6 educators. On August 16, at the invitation of third- through fifth-grade ESL instructor Michael Bowden, I presented one activity to 50 Lewisville I.S.D. second-grade through middle/high school educators. The constructive suggestions of these education professionals improved my activities.

Chess Equipment and Chess Curricula

Chess Equipment

For the activities in this book, one **board** and **set** is needed for every two students. Boards should have algebraic notation marked around the outside borders. In algebraic notation, **files** are labeled a–h, and **ranks** are labeled 1–8. As shown in Figure 1.4, a square is described file-first, followed by rank. Boards with notation are often sold in combination with a **Staunton** set. To meet tournament and teaching standards, yet keep costs low, match a solid-plastic set (with a **king** that measures 3.75 inches in height) with a 20-inch vinyl board. By ordering in quantity, the cost for each board and set combination works out to about $6. In Figure 1.5, my children are shown playing chess on such a set and board.

I recommend purchasing chess equipment from the USCF sales division http://www.uscfsales.com or from American Chess Equipment http://www.amchesseq.com/. Although it might be tempting to save money buying chess equipment at a local toy store, think again. Toy store boards lack algebraic notation markings, and their pieces are hollow plastic and therefore tip over easily.

Free chess equipment is available for qualified schools. The USCF Web site http://www.uschess.org has forms online about

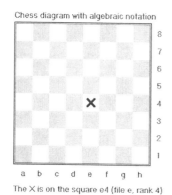

Chess diagram with algebraic notation

The X is on the square e4 (file e, rank 4)

Figure 1.4.
Square in algebraic notation.

Figure 1.5.
Clarissa and William Root using standard chess equipment.

the U.S. Chess Trust (501c3) Chess for Youth program. The Trust provides up to five sets and boards to start a school chess program. Additionally, Title I schools are eligible for up to 10 USCF memberships for needy students. One might also approach educational foundations with grant requests. Several of my "Chess in Education Certificate" online students have obtained grants to purchase chess books, software, and equipment. Successful grant applications demonstrate the benefits of chess to students, schools, and communities. Read Root (2006) for examples of the intersection of chess with educational goals.

Score sheets, for taking chess notation, are also useful. For younger students, score sheets must have large spaces for recording moves. Figure 1.6 is a custom-designed score sheet. Older students can substitute notebook paper for score sheets. If teaching more than eight students at once, invest in a **demonstration board** such as the one shown in Figure 1.7. The cost for a demonstration board with pieces and a carrying case is around $20 from American Chess Equipment.

If students will be competing in chess tournaments, purchase chess **clocks.** Most scholastic chess **tournament directors** expect students to operate chess clocks. In Figure 1.8, each player originally had 60 minutes to play all of his moves for the game. The clock faces show that around 30 of those minutes have already been used to arrive at the position on the board. Black's clock button is up, and his clock time is running, because it is his move. After he makes his move, he will push the button on the top of his clock to start his opponent's clock ticking. The clock shown is analog; higher-priced digital clocks more precisely display the time remaining for each side.

Chess Curricula

Many educators appreciate resources that teach the rules and basic strategies of chess, either as a supplement to teacher-created lessons or for stand-alone use. I list some titles in the References section. Other top choices are cited in Root (2006, pp. 109–110). Dewain Barber (2003, p. 23) categorized books and software for different chess levels; the rest of his free publication provides step-by-step instruction on how to run chess clubs and tournaments.

Several free resources introduce chess to school-age children. In 2006 foundations headed by former **World Champion** Garry Kasparov and by former Women's World Champion Susan Polgar released curricula that give teachers day-by-day chess lesson plans (Khmelnitsky, Khodarkovsky, & Zadorozny, 2006; Polgar, 2006; see Appendix C for a review of these curricula). The chessKIDS academy has self-paced chess

CHESS SCORE SHEET

White _____ Black _____

Result (circle what happened): white won, black won, draw

Date of game: _____

White	Black
1.	
2.	
3.	
4.	
5.	
6.	
7.	
8.	
9.	
10.	
11.	
12.	
13.	
14.	
15.	
16.	
17.	
18.	
19.	

White	Black
20.	
21.	
22.	
23.	
24.	
25.	
26.	
27.	
28.	
29.	
30.	
31.	
32.	
33.	
34.	
35.	
36.	
37.	
38.	

If the game goes beyond 38 moves, you may continue writing moves on the back of this score sheet.

Figure 1.6.
Chess score sheet.

From *Science, Math, Checkmate: 32 Chess Activities for Inquiry and Problem Solving* by Alexey W. Root. Westport, CT: Teacher Ideas Press. Copyright © 2008.

Figure 1.7.
Demonstration board.

lessons with interactive features at http://www.chesskids.com.

Other chess resources cost money. Schools aligned with America's Foundation for Chess (AF4C), http://www.af4c.org, gain support from chess mentors and the First Move curricula. Costs are shared between AF4C and the school. In 2007–2008, First Move will be used by 25,000 second- and third-grade students. The Think Like a King School Chess Software System, http://www.schoolchess.com/, starts with beginner lessons *(First Lessons in Chess)*. Its other CDs cover advanced chess topics to provide a comprehensive scholastic chess curriculum.

Organization of *Science, Math, Checkmate*

Chapters 2 (scientific inquiry), 3 (mathematical problem solving), and 4 (interdisciplinary) each contain 9–12 activities at different grade and chess levels. Within each chapter, activities are organized from least to most chess knowledge required. Chapter 5 gives the rules of chess and instruction on algebraic notation. Appendix A is the chess test and answer key. Appendix B has the answer key for the 32 chess activities in chapters 2–4 and for Figure 5.11. Appendix C reviews the curricula offered by the Kasparov and Polgar Chess Foundations. The glossary defines the chess terms used in the text. The References chapter has a chart of national standards addressed by the activities and gives bibliographic citations of all sources. The book ends with an index.

Chess Coding of Activities

Figure 1.8.
Chess clock.

The 32 activities in *Science, Math, Checkmate* are equally divided among grade levels and chess knowledge. "White" activities are for grades 3 through 5, and "black" activities are for grades 6 through 8. Chess levels are indicated by the 16 pawn, 4 knight, 4 **bishop,** 4 **rook,** 2 queen, and 2 king codes, with 1 code attached to each activity. The 16 pawn-coded activities require little or no chess knowledge. Figure 1.9 lists each activity in the book by grade level and by the amount of chess knowledge required to begin the activity.

For example, a black pawn (♟) means that the activity is for grades 6 through 8,

Chess code	Meaning of chess code	Activities
# of activities within code.	What each chess code designates, in terms of chess knowledge prerequisites.	The chapter in which the coded activities are located, followed by the names of the activities in that chapter. Chapter 2 = science, chapter 3 = math, chapter 4 = interdisciplinary.
♙/8 (eight white pawn-coded activities)	Little or no chess knowledge; grades 3–5.	Chapter 2: Physical Properties of Pieces; chapter 3: Covering the Board: Rooks; Perimeter and Surface Area of the Board; Balancing Chess Equations; Practice Producing Polygons; chapter 4: Learning Chess Pieces; Map My School on a Board; The Knights Can't Wait!
♟/8 (eight black pawn-coded activities)	Little or no chess knowledge; grades 6–8.	Chapter 2: Pawn Game; 3-on-3; chapter 3: Covering the Board: Kings; Eight Queens; Pawns, Pieces, Proportions, and Probability; Chess Players' Stats; Pick a Pocketful of Pieces; chapter 4: The King's Chessboard

Before beginning the piece-coded activities, use chapter 5 to teach or review algebraic notation, check, checkmate, stalemate, and the basic moves of pawns and pieces.

Chess code	Meaning of chess code	Activities
♘/2	Knowledge of chess rules except en passant and castling; grades 3–5.	Chapter 2: 20 Questions; Chapter 4: How to Castle
♞/2	Knowledge of chess rules except en passant and castling; grades 6–8.	Chapter 2: Black Box; Chapter 3: Mazes and Monsters
♗/2	Mastery of chess rules except en passant; grades 3–5.	Chapter 3: Working Backward; Chapter 4: Kasparov versus the World
♝/2	Mastery of chess rules except en passant; grades 6–8.	Chapter 2: Computers and Checkmates; To e.p. or not to e.p.
♖/2	Mastery of all chess rules and the ability to solve one-move chess problems; grades 3–5.	Chapter 2: Criteria Challenge; Chess Models
♜/2	Mastery of all chess rules and the ability to solve one-move chess problems; grades 6–8.	Chapter 3: Transforming Figures; Chapter 4: Know More, Move More!
♕/1	Familiarity with basic chess strategies and the ability to solve some two-move chess problems; grades 3–5.	Chapter 4: Move Order Mystery
♛/1	Familiarity with basic chess strategies and the ability to solve some two-move chess problems; grades 6–8.	Chapter 4: Openings around the World

Chess code	Meaning of chess code	Activities
♔/1	Familiarity with multiple chess strategies and the ability to solve two-move chess problems; grades 3–5.	Chapter 2: The Good Bishop
♚/1	Familiarity with multiple chess strategies and the ability to solve two-move chess problems; grades 6–8.	Chapter 2: Stalemate Surprise

Figure 1.9.
Key to chess coding of activities.

From *Science, Math, Checkmate: 32 Chess Activities for Inquiry and Problem Solving* by Alexey W. Root. Westport, CT: Teacher Ideas Press. Copyright © 2008.

with little or no knowledge of chess. A white knight (♘) designates the activity as appropriate for third through fifth graders who have knowledge of the chess rules except for en passant and castling. Before starting the piece-coded activities, use chapter 5 (or other beginner's chess text or software) to teach algebraic notation, **check,** checkmate, stalemate, and most of the rules of chess.

Chess Test

At this point, you may choose to administer the chess test in Appendix A. To shorten the test for younger students, split it into two or three parts. Tell students, "This test is to see how much you already know about chess. Don't worry if you get the answers wrong; I will go over the right answers with you. If some of the answers are confusing right now, they will become clearer as you learn more about chess during our chess activities." The answers for the test are also in Appendix A. After assessing your students' answers to the test, you will have a better sense of their chess knowledge. If the students answer the pawn-level questions correctly, you may start with either the pawn-level or the piece-level activities. If you don't give the test, or if students miss a lot of questions on the test, start on the 16 pawn-level activities and use chapter 5 to prepare your students for the 16 piece-level activities.

The test scores achieved predict how easy the chess content of the activities will be for your students, but not how well they will comprehend the science and math content of the activities. In other words, a student who scores perfectly on the test may learn quite a bit about science or math (but not much about chess) from a pawn-level activity. At the end of your chess instruction, you may administer the chess test again as a post-test.

The activities in chapters 2–4 and the chess basics in chapter 5 give students a great chess start. Learning by playing will accelerate their chess progress. If possible, have sets and boards handy for indoor recess, for free periods, for before and after school, and during lunch. Although some students already have, or will soon gain, a high level of chess-playing strength, students of all chess levels will enjoy the activities in *Science, Math, Checkmate.* The connections of chess to science, math, and other academic content will intrigue chess novices along with chess veterans. Improved thinking in science, math, and chess will result.

Chapter 2

SCIENTIFIC INQUIRY

Connections to Science Standards

According to Tim Redman, who was the director of the UTD Chess Program from 1996 to 2006, chess and science share important connections. What follows is my paraphrase of his "Chess as Science" online lecture:

Chess world champion (1948–1957; 1958–1960; 1961–1963) Mikhail Botvinnik was an electrical engineer, computer programmer, and chess school founder in his USSR homeland. He advocated a scientific approach to chess. Chess world champion Emanuel Lasker (1894–1921) was a friend of Albert Einstein, with whom he discussed the theory of relativity. German players of the late nineteenth and early twentieth century, such as world champion Steinitz (1886–1894) and Aron Nimzovich, attempted to define the scientific laws of the game of chess. To what extent can chess be considered a science?

Chess players try to learn, test, and discover general laws governing chess play. Most people would not consider chess players scientists because chess is self-referential. The latest innovation in a chess opening will never contribute to our knowledge of the world or our ability to manipulate it. Chess makes nothing happen, except more chess.

Nevertheless, the study and play of chess resembles the study and play of science. Chess and science are both logical; they are both absorbing occupations; they both involve a systematic accumulation of knowledge based on hypothesis and testing. So perhaps it can be said that chess is much like a science. (T. Redman, personal communication, 2001)

The activities in this chapter engage students as chess player-scientists, testing their ideas about chess with observations, hypotheses, and experiments. Answers are provided, sometimes within the activity and more often in Appendix B. These answers, when revealed to the students, are meaningful because students have attempted the activity. Sometimes teachers should give partial answers, or hints, during the activity. As stated in the National Science Education Standards,

Although open exploration is useful for students when they encounter new materials and phenomena, teachers need to intervene to focus and challenge the students, or the exploration might not lead to understanding. Premature intervention deprives students of the opportunity to confront problems and find solutions, but intervention that occurs too late risks student frustration. (National Research Council, 1996, p. 36)

♟ Physical Properties of Pieces

This activity is an edited version of a lesson plan written by James W. Williams, Detroit Public Schools, April, 2007.

Objectives: Students identify the natural resources used to make sets. Students identify these resources as renewable, nonrenewable, or reusable.

Prior to attempting this activity, students should be able to classify common natural resources as renewable, reusable, or nonrenewable. Students should also be familiar with the properties of those resources.

Materials: For the teacher, an overhead projector and one copy of Figure 2.1 on a transparency. For each student, one photocopy of Figure 2.1 and a pencil. For each group of students, a balance scale, a magnet, a small container with water (large enough to put a chess piece in), a numbered bag, and numbered chess pieces made of different materials for each bag. Each bag should have six pawns and pieces of roughly the same size made of, for example, stone, wood, plastic, metal, clay, and glass. Chess pieces might come from students' sets from home, from garage sales, flea markets, and so forth. Since complete sets of chess pieces are not needed, this activity is a great way to use old sets with missing pieces. If fewer chess pieces are available for each bag, evaluate less than six pieces on Figure 2.1.

Procedure: Begin with a brief overview of the history of chess. The game is believed to have originated in India over 1,500 years ago. Some of the pieces were different from the pieces used today. For example, the rooks were chariots and the bishops were elephants. Ask students to speculate what materials were used to make these original pieces. Stone, clay, and animal bone are all possibilities. Accept all reasonable answers. Tell the students that today they will study chess pieces

Name _____ Date_____

PHYSICAL PROPERTIES CHART

Directions: Check off or complete each chart entry that applies to each piece in your group's bag.

My group had bag number _____.

Piece Number	clear	opaque	shiny	dull	color	Weight	Float	Sink	Magnet Attracts
1									
2									
3									
4									
5									
6									

After observing the six pieces this is my conclusion:

Piece 1 is made out of _____, which is a _____ resource.

Piece 2 is made out of _____, which is a _____ resource.

Piece 3 is made out of _____, which is a _____ resource.

Piece 4 is made out of _____, which is a _____resource.

Piece 5 is made out of _____, which is a _____resource.

Piece 6 is made out of _____, which is a _____resource.

Figure 2.1.
Physical Properties Chart.

From *Science, Math, Checkmate: 32 Chess Activities for Inquiry and Problem Solving* by Alexey W. Root. Westport, CT: Teacher Ideas Press. Copyright © 2008.

made out of six different materials. Students will use their knowledge of physical properties of matter to determine which material was used to make each piece. Direct their attention to the overhead projector. Demonstrate how to evaluate the first piece from one of the bags. Fill in the overhead transparency chart (Figure 2.1) while completing the following five steps:

1. Show what number bag you have to the class. Fill in the bag number on Figure 2.1 transparency. Explain that each bag will have six pieces, but that some bags have bigger pieces than others.
2. Continue observing the piece using the sense of sight and check off the appropriate chart entries (boxes on the chart). Be sure to explain the term *opaque* as it might be new to your students.
3. Weigh the piece on a balance scale and record the weight.
4. Place the piece in water and record whether it floats or sinks.
5. Place the piece near a magnet and record whether the piece is attracted by the magnet.

Pass out a physical properties chart to the students. Assign students to work in groups of two to four students, passing out one bag of pieces to each of the groups. Have a central area for one representative of each group to pick up the scales, containers of water, and magnets. Students should take turns evaluating pieces in their groups. Students work together, agreeing about each answer before they actually check it off. Circulate to make sure that all the groups are working productively.

Evaluation: Students use the data from the chart at the top of Figure 2.1 and their prior knowledge to predict what material each piece was made from and to identify each material as a renewable, nonrenewable, or reusable resource. Students should turn in their charts to be checked for accuracy and completeness. A sample answer key is in Appendix B, though actual answers will vary based on the materials used for this exercise. The activity could be repeated by having the groups exchange bags and fill out fresh copies of Figure 2.1.

♟ Pawn Game

Objectives: Students learn the **legal** moves of a pawn, with the option to learn the special moves of promotion and en passant. Students record data from four trials of the pawn game. After the four trials, students share data and hypotheses in a whole class discussion.

Materials: Chess demonstration board, set and board for every two students, class set of Figure 2.2, class set of Figure 2.4, one pencil or pen for each student. If the special pawn moves of promotion and en passant will be taught during this lesson, class set of Figure 2.3. For other instructional examples of the pawn game, see Basman (2001, p. 15);

RULES FOR PAWN MOVES—BASIC MOVES

Pawns move one or two squares on their initial move, but only one square at a time after that initial move. In Diagram 1, the white pawn (WP) could move to e3 or e4, but the black pawn (BP) on b6 (which had previously made an initial move from b7-b6) may move to b5, not to b4.

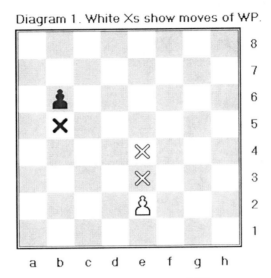

Diagram 1. White Xs show moves of WP.

Black X shows legal move of BP.

Diagram 2 shows that pawns capture along the diagonal. It is white to move in Diagram 2. The WP on e4 and the BP on e5 are blocking each other. However, the WP on f4 could capture the BP on e5 or it could move one square forward to f5. If it were instead black to move, the BP on e5 has only one legal move: to capture the WP on f4. When a pawn capture is made, the enemy pawn is removed and the capturing pawn sits on its vacated square.

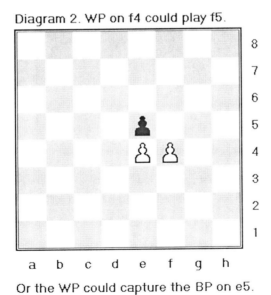

Diagram 2. WP on f4 could play f5.

Or the WP could capture the BP on e5.

Figure 2.2.
Basic pawn moves.

From *Science, Math, Checkmate: 32 Chess Activities for Inquiry and Problem Solving* by Alexey W. Root. Westport, CT: Teacher Ideas Press. Copyright © 2008.

RULES FOR PAWN MOVES—SPECIAL MOVES

Diagram 3 illustrates promotion, one of the two special moves that pawns have in a chess game. When a white pawn (WP) reaches the eighth rank, or a black pawn (BP) reaches the first rank, the pawn becomes either a Queen (Q), Rook (R), Bishop (B) or Knight (N). The notation for promotion is written d1(Q) if the BP promotes to a queen. If the WP in Diagram 3 promotes to a knight, the notation would read f8(N).

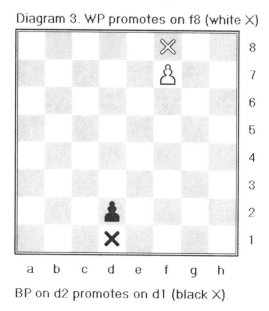

Diagram 3. WP promotes on f8 (white X)

BP on d2 promotes on d1 (black X).

The other special move, en passant, is illustrated in Diagram 4. When an enemy pawn (on f7 the move before the position shown in Diagram 4) double-jumps to a square (f5) located on a file and rank adjacent to your pawn (e5), you can capture that pawn as if it only moved one square. If you want to capture en passant (exf6 e.p.), you must make that capture immediately or the option is no longer available for that pawn duo. In Diagram 4, after exf6 e.p., your white pawn would sit on f6 and the black pawn would be removed from the board.

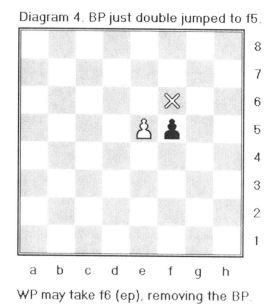

Diagram 4. BP just double jumped to f5.

WP may take f6 (ep), removing the BP.

Figure 2.3.
Special pawn moves.

From *Science, Math, Checkmate: 32 Chess Activities for Inquiry and Problem Solving* by Alexey W. Root. Westport, CT: Teacher Ideas Press. Copyright © 2008.

Name _____

PAWN GAME DATA SHEET

Starting position for the pawn game.

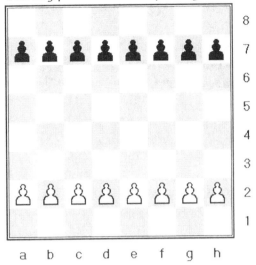

White moves first.

Fill out the following data table as you play the Pawn (P) Game. Play the game four times, twice with the white pawns and twice with the black pawns. White wins if a white pawn reaches the eighth rank. Black wins if a black pawn reaches the first rank. A win is also recorded if one side captures all the opponent's pawns. A draw occurs when neither side can move (pawns are blocked).

Pawn Game Trial #	# of Ps captured by white?	# of Ps captured by black?	Win, loss, or draw for white?	Why do you think the result happened?
1				
2				
3				
4				

Figure 2.4.
Data sheet for Pawn Game.

From *Science, Math, Checkmate: 32 Chess Activities for Inquiry and Problem Solving* by Alexey W. Root. Westport, CT: Teacher Ideas Press. Copyright © 2008.

Khmelnitsky, Khodarkovsky, and Zadorozny (2006, Book 1, pp. 32–47); MacEnulty (2006, p. 122); Polgar (2006, p. 3); and Pelts and Alburt (1992, p. 5).

Procedure: Teach or review the legal moves of the pawn, including how it **captures,** using Figure 2.2 as your instructional guide. If you have a long class period, teach pawn promotion and the en passant capture before starting the pawn game.

Explain that students will play the pawn game four times, twice with the white pawns and twice with the black pawns. For each of the four trials of the pawn game, students will record on Figure 2.4 the number of pawns captured by white, the number of pawns captured by black, the result of the game, and why they believe that result occurred. A win is awarded to the side that: (1) captures all of the opponent's pawns, or (2) first promotes a pawn. A draw, or tie, is the result when all the pawns block each other and no legal moves are possible. Ask students to raise their hands during the activity if they are unsure about a pawn move or rule, so that you can assist them.

Pair up students, and pass out one board and set to each pair. Give one copy of Figure 2.2, Figure 2.4, and (optional) Figure 2.3 to each student. If the promotion and en passant rules were not taught, tell students that those rules won't be used today and don't pass out Figure 2.3. Remind students to record data each time that they play the pawn game, up to four trials, on Figure 2.4. Ask students to play **touch move,** explain the touch-move rule, and state that it cuts down on disputes about what move is intended.

Tell students that they are scientists, not just chess opponents. They are working together to figure out the underlying principles of the pawn game. If pairs of students finish four trials before their classmates, they may play additional trials of the pawn game for fun.

Evaluation: After each pair has had a chance to play the pawn game four times, pack up the sets, the boards, and the photocopies of Figure 2.2 and Figure 2.3. Ask whether students played cooperatively with their opponents during the pawn game, following the touch move rule. Discuss any problems in sportsmanship, either that you observed or that students mention, and how those might be addressed. Ask students to show thumbs up for legal moves or thumbs down for **illegal** moves as you show various pawn moves and captures on the demonstration board. Review the en passant and promotion rules if those were taught. Remember that the pawn game was a first introduction to chess, so look for good effort rather than perfect execution of chess rules.

If time is short, delay sharing data from Figure 2.4 until a later class period. At that time, have each pair of students share one typical trial from columns one through four of Figure 2.4. Record their data on the dry-erase board. Ask students to look for patterns in the data. When white captured more pawns in a particular trial, did white win? When white and black captured equal amounts of pawns, was the result a draw? Ask students to

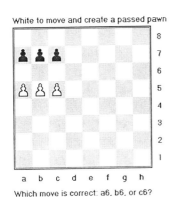

Figure 2.5.
Solving the 3-on-3 problem.

look at the fourth column, their hypotheses for each result. One likely hypothesis is that creating a **passed pawn** means that one will likely win the pawn game. Return to the pawn game activity several times during the school year, to practice pawn moves, en passant, and promotion.

♟ 3-on-3

Objectives: Students understand the 3-on-3 pawn **problem,** make a plan, carry out the plan, and prove whether the resulting position met the plan's goal. Students learn that the **sacrifice** of **material** is justified to promote a pawn. Students practice making best moves, which correspond to ideal conditions in science experiments. Students learn the term "passed pawn."

Materials: Demonstration board. Set and board for every two students, class sets of Figure 2.2 and Figure 2.3. Polgar (2006, p. 4), Eade (2005, pp. 235–237), Pandolfini (1995, p. 53), and USCF and Kurzdorfer (2003, p. 133) also demonstrate this 3-on-3 pawn position and its solution. Figure 2.5 shows students solving the 3-on-3 problem.

Procedure: Teach or review the legal moves of the pawn, including how pawns capture and promote. Either lecture about pawn moves from the demonstration board and/or pass out Figure 2.2 and Figure 2.3. En passant, covered in Figure 2.3, won't apply in the 3-on-3 activity. But promotion, also covered in Figure 2.3, is a part of this activity. Display Figure 2.6 on the demonstration board. Define a passed pawn as having no enemy pawn opposing it on its own file or on an adjacent file. The goal for white is to create a passed pawn, since that passed pawn will promote before a black pawn promotes. Tell students that promotion isn't a win in a chess game; checkmate is. Nevertheless, promoting a pawn in a chess game often leads to a win. When one promotes, one usually asks for a queen. Adding such a powerful piece to one's chess forces is often enough to win the game.

Ask students to indicate all of white's possible first moves in Figure 2.6: 1. a6, or 1. b6, or 1. c6. Play 1. a6 on the demonstration board. Ask if black should respond by 1....c6. Students should respond no, because then white would play 2. axb7 and be one move away from promoting and winning the activity. Instruct students that, when playing this position out with a partner, both sides must play what they consider best moves. If black plays a poor move, as just

White to move and create a passed pawn

Which move is correct: a6, b6, or c6?

Figure 2.6.
3-on-3 pawn problem position.

shown, then the conclusions reached won't be valid. One comparison might be to a science experiment where the experimenter makes lots of errors: measuring incorrectly, observing inaccurately, and rushing the procedure. Ask students if such an experiment would yield reliable conclusions. (Answer: No.)

Ask each pair of students to test each of white's first moves. Students should determine which first move, when followed by second and third moves, creates a passed pawn. Pass out boards and sets, and allow students to play out the position for 10–15 minutes. Remind them to think before they move, and to play with the touch move rule. Pack up boards, sets, and Figures 2.2 and 2.3 before the whole class discussion at the end of the activity.

Evaluation: Observe students' play for thoughtfulness and following the touch-move rule. If any of the pairs arrive at the solutions, allow those pairs to show their solutions on the demonstration board at the end of the activity. The answer key for 3-on-3 is in Appendix B.

♞ 20 Questions

Objective: Students ask and answer 20 questions to determine the identities of mystery chess pieces and pawns.

Materials: Dry-erase board. Paper and pen for each team. Optional: demonstration board.

Procedure: At the beginning of the student activity, recite and write on the dry-erase board the names of the chess figures: king (K), queen (Q), rook (R), bishop (B), knight (N), and pawn (P). Then call on various students to tell how each piece and pawn moves and captures, and the value of each in **points.** If desired, students can be called up to the demonstration board to show the legal moves of each piece and pawn. Correct any student errors. Ask how many different types of chess figures are on the board at the start of the game. The students answer "six." Then ask students to take the color of the chess figure into account. The answer is now 12 unique figures, as follows: ♔ ♚ ♕ ♛ ♖ ♜ ♗ ♝ ♘ ♞ ♙ ♟

Share the rules of 20 questions. The class will be divided into two teams, splitting the room in half. Team two writes the name and color of a piece or pawn on a piece of paper, and shows that paper to the teacher but not to team one. Members of team one then take turns asking yes or no questions to figure out which piece or pawn is written on team two's paper. Team one members can consult in between asking questions, but a different team member must ask each question. A team two spokesperson, new for each turn, answers the yes or no questions asked by team one. Alternatively, team two can answer in unison. On the dry-erase board, the teacher keeps track of how many questions were asked by team one. When the team one correctly guesses the mystery piece or pawn, its remaining questions are held over for round two. Then team one thinks of a mystery piece or pawn, and team two asks questions to discover its identity.

Here is a sample round one. The team two thinks of a white rook. Team one, member one asks, "Is the piece white?" Team two answers, "Yes." The teacher tallies one on the board. Member two of team one asks, "Can the piece hop over other pieces?" Team two answers, "No," and the teacher makes a second tally mark on the board. Member three (of team one) asks, "Is it a white queen?" Team two answers, "No," and the teacher makes a third tally on the board. Thus the count now stands at 17 questions remaining for team one for this round and all future rounds. Member four of team one asks, "Can the piece move horizontally?" Team two says, "Yes," and the tally total is at four (16 questions remaining). Member five of team one asks, "Can the piece move multiple squares at a time?" Team two responds, "Yes," and the tally total is five (15 questions remaining). Member six of team one asks, "Is it a white rook?" and team one has survived round one and has 14 questions remaining for future rounds. It is now team two's turn, so team one writes a chess figure and prepares to answer questions.

Evaluation: Teams should be complimented for the number of rounds they can play with their 20 questions. Both teams may run out of questions on the same round, so ties are possible. Pay attention to the quality of questions asked and whether the questions are answered accurately. In the example given, a poor second question would have been, "Is the piece black?" Member four asked a very good question by using the word "horizontally." Other than the queen, who had already been eliminated as an answer, only the rook and king move horizontally. Member five eliminated the king answer by asking about multiple squares per move. Therefore, member six knew that the answer was a rook (because of the answers to members four and five) and, more specifically, a white rook (because of the answer to member one).

Figure 2.7.
Jeff Ashton teaching black box.

Black Box

This activity is an edited version of a blog posting written by Jeffrey Ashton, USCF National Master, http://schoolof-chess.blogspot.com/, April 18, 2007.

Objectives: Through use of a stimulus and response procedure, students figure out where a king is hidden. Students compare the procedures for finding the king to investigating the black box in science.

Materials: Demonstration board, one board and pieces for every two students, paper, pencils.

Procedure: Tell students the story of science being like the black box. One can't open the black box or reach in it but other types of input or stimuli are possible. A scientist might shake the box or puncture it with sticks. Then there will be output or responses: the sound of the rattling inside the box or the sensation of the stick hitting an object in the box. After repeated input and output, also called an investigation, a scientist formulates a model about what is in the black box. Another analogy is the behavior of children before a holiday: Told not to unwrap presents, they instead shake or prod them to guess what's inside.

Give the rules for the black box chess game. Figure 2.7 shows Jeff Ashton teaching the black box rules. The game can be played with two players per side, or one player per side. One consideration for having two students on the investigative side is that they could collaborate to select the best possible input. The black box side hides their king by writing the notation of the king's square without placing the king on the board. The investigative side uses its king, queen, two rooks, two bishops, and two knights, beginning by placing one of those pieces on a square. After that placement, the black box side says either "hit" (check) or "miss" depending on whether or not the move checked the king. The round continues until the investigative side has used all its pieces. Then the hits for the round are totaled. One tricky part of the game is that if the king's mystery square is e4, and the move by the other side placed a piece on e4, then the black box side indicates a miss even though the piece has landed on the king.

Play a sample game on the demonstration board, with you taking the black box side and the class taking the investigative side. For the purposes of this demonstration, let's hide your black king on a8. Write a8 on a piece of paper, but don't physically put your king on the demonstration board. Also, don't change its position in response to hits (checks). White, played by the class, announces 1. Qe4. You respond "hit," because your king is in check. Now the class tries 2. Rh4, thinking that your king is on the fourth rank. You respond "miss." The class plays 3. Bf3, which would be a check if there were not a queen blocking the line to the king. You respond "miss." The class now plays 4. Bb5. You respond "miss." Although normally one can have just one light-squared bishop per game, in black box you can have bishops of the same color as in **bughouse.** The class plays 5. Kd8, and you respond "miss." The class plays 6. Rc8 and you respond, "hit." Having realized where your king is hiding, the class plays 7. Nc7 another "hit" and 8. Nb6, also a "hit." At this point, reveal the king's location by placing it on the demonstration board. Count up the hits. Figure 2.8 shows the total number of hits that the class earned for this round.

White hit (checked) 4 times.

White missed (didn't check) 4 times.

Figure 2.8.
Sample black box final position.

Arrange students in groups for three rounds of black box. Each side plays the lone king three times, and the investigative side three times. Players should track total hits per round. The winner is the side that gets the most hits over all three rounds.

Evaluation: Circulate as the groups play black box. Ask students how they decided what inputs to use, that is, where to put their **attacking** pieces. Also ask students if they had a strategy for where to hide the king. Jeff Ashton noted that students often give away the location of their king by staring at the king's spot on the board. After the first day of playing black box, discuss whether clues such as eye movement helped players figure out the location of the hidden, black box, king. If so, can this be compared to scientists' black box investigations?

♟ Computers and Checkmates

Objectives: Using the Internet or a software program, students learn how to checkmate with a king and queen against a lone king. Students recognize that stalemating is a less desirable result than checkmating for the side with the queen. Students' computer use complements the science inquiry standard for grades 5 through 8, "The use of computers for the collection, summary, and display of evidence is part of this standard" (National Research Council, 1996, p. 145).

Materials: One board and set for every two students. If possible, allow one computer per student with Internet access or chess software. Child-friendly sites that teach the king and queen mate are the chessKIDS academy http://www.chesskids.com/level2/cl4l7.htm, and chess-poster. com http://www.chess-poster.com/chess_problems/mate_king_queen. htm. Find additional sites by entering the terms "king queen checkmate" into a search engine. Screen the results to make sure they are appropriate for your students. The Think Like a King School Chess Software System, *First Lessons in Chess* CD, has a section on the king and queen against king mate. To prepare for your lecture, visit the previously mentioned Internet sites or Chess Corner http://www.chesscorner.com/tutorial/basic/q_mate/q_mate.htm, or use chess software.

If computers are not available, prepare for your lecture by reading a chess beginner book with instructions on how to checkmate with king and queen versus king. Some examples are: Pelts and Alburt (1992, pp. 65–68); Polgar (2006, pp. 23–24); or Khmelnitsky, Khodarkovsky, and Zadorozny (2006, Book 1, pp. 125–137). Optional: **diagram** (chess diagram) program such as DiagTransfer, http://alain.blaisot.free.fr/DiagTransfer/English/ home.htm.

Procedure: Ask students for some of the uses of computers in science. Students might answer that computers store data, allow practice of techniques (such as virtual surgery), and facilitate communication of scientific results via email and the Internet. Tell students that today they will be collecting evidence from a computer, and then using what they've learned to checkmate a fellow student in a practice drill.

Teach students how to checkmate with a king and queen against a king. A great method of instruction is for students to learn and to practice the mate with Internet sites or with chess software as listed in the materials section of this activity.

If students do not have computer access during the activity, show the mate on the demonstration board instead. Mention that you used the computer (if you visited the Internet sites or used chess software) to prepare your lecture. If you didn't previously know how to complete this checkmate, tell students about your experience learning from the computer. Ask students to share how learning from interactive software or Internet sites differs from learning from books or documents.

Pass out a set and board to each pair of students. Each student should take three turns defending with the lone king (which should be placed in the **center** of the board so that checkmating it takes several moves) and three turns checkmating with the king and queen side.

Evaluation: To continue the computer theme of this lesson, have students prepare either a Power Point or other document summarizing how to checkmate with a king and queen against king. To enhance the students' documents, make available a diagram-making program such as DiagTransfer, http://alain.blaisot.free.fr/DiagTransfer/English/home. htm, which has a free download.

♟ To e.p. or not to e.p.

Objectives: Students learn when it is possible to play en passant (e.p.), and when e.p. is not possible. Students compare the conditions of when e.p. is possible to conditions that precipitate a metamorphosis.

Materials: Demonstration board, class set of Figure 2.9, pencils, dry-erase board.

Procedure: Review a middle-school science lesson where certain conditions allow an action to occur. For example, geologists list three types of rocks: igneous, sedimentary, and metamorphous. Igneous or sedimentary rocks may turn into metamorphous rocks under conditions of high temperature and pressure. If the conditions aren't there, the rocks don't change type.

In chess, conditions for en passant occur in less than 1 game out of 10 (USCF & Kurzdorfer, 2003, p. 62). When a white pawn is on the algebraically labeled fifth rank or a black pawn is on the algebraically labeled fourth rank, it may capture (using the en passant rule) an enemy pawn that double jumps on an adjacent file. If the e.p. option is not immediately exercised, then the double-jumping pawn is safe from the e.p. capture. A white pawn capturing e.p. lands on the sixth rank and a black pawn capturing e.p. lands on the third rank, in both cases on the same file as the captured enemy pawn. That enemy pawn is removed from the board.

Name _____

Write the notation of the en passant capture in the space provided under the diagram. If the en passant capture is not possible, explain why not in the space below the diagram. Some questions require a yes or no answer. Remember, the en passant capture is optional. The diagrams are all from the same chess game, so answer #1 first, then #2, then #3, then #4.

#1: Black's move. White played 1. c2-c4.

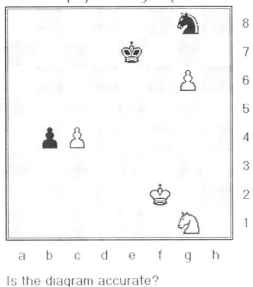

If black can e.p., write the notation

1.... _____

#2: White's move. Black played 1....g7-g5

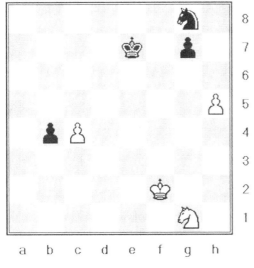

If white can e.p., write the notation

2.... _____

#3: White played 2. hxg6 e.p.

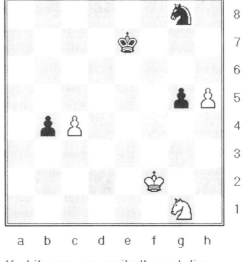

Is the diagram accurate?

_____

#4: Black's move.

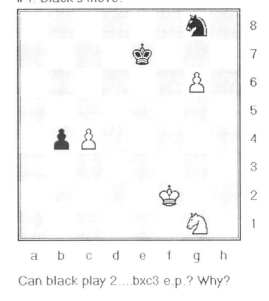

Can black play 2....bxc3 e.p.? Why?

_____

Figure 2.9.
En passant (e.p.).

From *Science, Math, Checkmate: 32 Chess Activities for Inquiry and Problem Solving* by Alexey W. Root. Westport, CT: Teacher Ideas Press. Copyright © 2008.

On the demonstration board, show the following moves. As you show the moves, indicated by **boldface,** write the notation on a dry-erase board. That way, students learn the notation for e.p. too. **1. e4 Nf6 2. e5 Ng8** (more common is 2....Nd5, the Alekhine's **Defense.** Explain that you are showing these moves not because they are best, but to illustrate how en passant arises in a game.) **3. d4 d5 4. exd6 e.p.** Remove the black pawn on d5 from the board. If you like, give the history of the e.p. rule as summarized in chapter 5. Continue the game **4....exd6 5. d5 c5** Ask students what white can do in this position. They should mention several options, such as 6. Nf3 (**developing** the N), 6. Bb5+ (developing the bishop), and 6. dxc6 e.p. Let's pretend that white chose **6. Nc3**, and black responded **6....Nf6** Now ask the class if white can play 7. dxc6 e.p. The answer is no, because e.p. must be played in the half-move immediately after an opponent's double-jump pawn move.

Evaluation: Pass out copies of Figure 2.9 to students. Tell students that all four positions on Figure 2.9 are from the same chess game, with each diagram representing a subsequent move. Correct the worksheet together when everyone has finished, asking students to write in the correct answers for questions missed. The answer key for Figure 2.9 is in Appendix B.

The next activity, Criteria Challenge, is analogous to science/engineering projects in which students are handed materials and told to make a product that meets certain specifications. For example, students might be handed toothpicks and glue and be instructed to build a weight-bearing bridge.

♜ Criteria Challenge

Objectives: Students work together to create chess positions that meet criteria. Students individually judge whether positions met the criteria and if they were presented well by their creators.

Materials: Four challenges written on dry-erase board; one set and board, and one copy of Figure 2.10 (optional), for every three to four students. Pencil and scratch paper for each student. A source for more chess challenges is the test section of volume one of Pelts and Alburt (1992, pp. 75–124).

Procedure: Write four challenges on the dry-erase board that are of the format "Place [these specific] pieces and pawns on the board in such a way that black is in, or a half-move away from, [checkmate or stalemate]." Challenge one: Place a white queen, white king, two black rooks, and the black king on the board in such a way that black is checkmated. (I added a white king to this Pelts and Alburt challenge.) Challenge two: Place the white king, a white bishop, the black king, a black bishop, and a black pawn on the board in such a way that black is stalemated (Pelts & Alburt, 1992, p. 75). Challenge three: Using any pieces and pawns that you want, make up a position where white can checkmate black by playing pawn takes pawn en passant (p. 77). Challenge four: Place a black king,

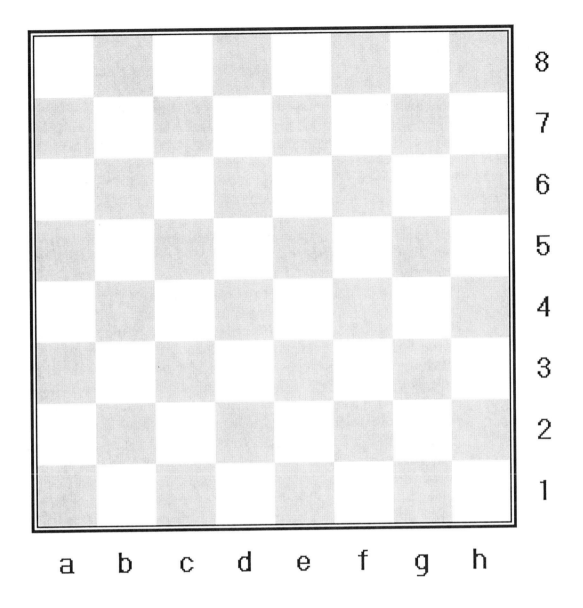

To make a diagram of a position, use the following abbreviations: P for white pawn, N for white knight, B for white bishop, R for white rook, Q for white queen, and K for white king. For example, a white rook on e4 is recorded by a letter R written on the e4 square.

Use the same abbreviations for black pieces and pawns, but circle them to show that a black piece or pawn is represented. For example, black rook on e6 is recorded by a ® [a circled letter R] on e6.

Figure 2.10.
Blank diagram for recording chess positions.

black pawn, white king, and white knight on the board in such a way that black is checkmated (p. 81).

Organize the students in groups of four. If there is a number not divisible by four, some groups should have three or two members rather than four. Each group should select one of the challenges from the dry-erase board. Mention that the en passant challenge is probably the hardest, since it requires planning a half-move ahead. Tell the groups that they have seven minutes to think of a position, create it on the chess board, and select a group name. An optional part of the plan is to ask each group to record its position on Figure 2.10, to have a permanent record of each group's work and to have a back-up if the chess position gets knocked over. Also during the seven minutes, groups may create campaigns, including chants, to convince classmates to vote for their challenge position.

After the seven minutes have elapsed, two representatives from each group of four (or one representative from each group of three or two) rotate to the other group's challenges. These visitors should carry a pencil and a piece of scratch paper. Each group informs the visitors which challenge was attempted and tells why their solution to the challenge is appealing. Each visitor writes private notes about which group most impressed and why, and decides on the group that will earn his or her vote. After the visitors return to their home position, the students who had been sitting home circulate. After everyone has visited all the groups, each person votes for the group that he or she felt best met the challenge attempted and, at the same time, best promoted their solution. Write the name of each group on the dry-erase board and ask for a show of hands in support of each group. Remind students to vote for the group that impressed them earlier, not simply for a group that seems to be winning the vote tally. Students may not vote for their own group.

This activity could be repeated multiple times by:

1. Creating four new challenges;
2. Your students making up challenges; or
3. Taking challenge positions from Pelts and Alburt (1992).

Evaluation: Look over the challenge positions as they are being created to see if they meet the criteria. A sample answer key is in Appendix B.

♜ Chess Models

Objectives: Students make analogies between models in science and models in chess. Models in science help scientists and the public comprehend complicated real-life phenomena. **Tactics** learned from a chess model help students solve a chess problem from a **grandmaster** game.

Materials: Demonstration board. Students should have notebook paper and a pencil. Optional: one set and board for every two students and additional photocopied problems from Pandolfini (1991).

Procedure: Quote from the national science education standards:

> Models are tentative schemes or structures that correspond to real objects, events, or classes of events, and that have explanatory power. Models help scientists and engineers understand how things work. Models take many forms, including physical objects, plans, mental constructs, mathematical equations, and computer simulations. (National Research Council, 1996, p. 117)

Ask students to name a model that they've used in class recently. For example, the class may have studied the solar system by making a chart, mobile, or diorama of the planets and their moons. Discuss that the model was a simplified version of the actual solar system. Review how the model was helpful for understanding the solar system. For example, the model might have shown the comparative sizes of the planets and the number of moons that orbit each planet.

Display Figure 2.11 on the demonstration board, explaining that the position is a model of a checkmate in one from an actual game. Ask students to write the solution. Walk around the room to see if students write 1....fxg3#, the solution given in Appendix B. After a couple of minutes, give hints until everyone has written the correct answer. Then set up Figure 2.12 on the demonstration board. Say, "The position on the demonstration board [Figure 2.12] is from the 1989 British Championship of chess. White was G. Burgess, and black was W. Watson. It is black's turn, and black can checkmate in two moves. The checkmate uses the same theme as our earlier, model problem."

If a limited chess activity is planned, don't pass out chess equipment or additional problems. Instead, have students solve the problem mentally while looking at the demonstration board. If additional problems are planned from Pandolfini (1991), those problems should be handed out now with the sets and boards. At this point, pairs of students could set up Figure 2.12 and then continue on to the other Pandolfini problems.

Whether limited or extensive problem solving is planned, each student should write his or her solution to each problem. After Figure 2.12 and whatever additional chess problems have been attempted or solved by students, show the solution(s) from Appendix B on the demonstration board. Discuss how first studying the model helped students solve the game's problem. Return to the discussion of a science model and a real-life science problem. How does a model that shows the planets' sizes and their moons' orbits help us understand whether or not Pluto is a planet?

Black to move and checkmate.

Pandolfini (1991, pp. 187, 193)...fxg3#.

Figure 2.11.

Black to move and checkmate.

2-move solution, Pandolfini (1991, p. 21)

Figure 2.12.

Under each diagram, write the best move for white and give the reason (A, B, or C) for your choice: A) The bishop limits the knight, now or in the near future. B) The bishop attacks the enemy pawns, now or in the near future. C) The position is open, making the bishop better than the knight.

Diagram 1.

White to move.

Diagram 2.

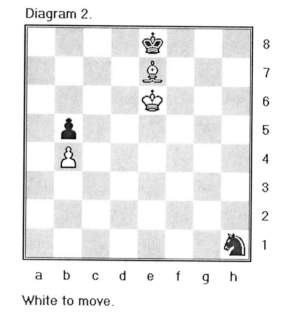

White to move.

Diagram 3.

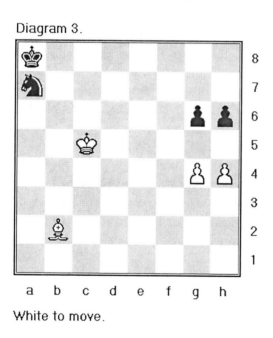

White to move.

Diagram 4.

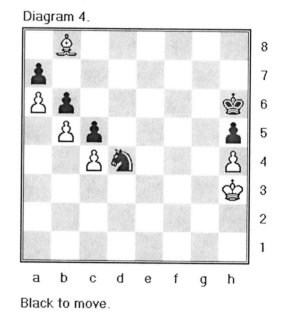

Black to move.

Figure 2.13.
The Good Bishop versus the Bad Knight.

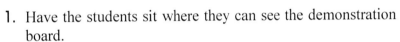

Evaluation: Ask students to write a paragraph about how models help us understand phenomena. Tell students that the paragraph should include examples from chess and from science.

♔ The Good Bishop

This activity is an edited version of a lesson plan written by Alex Chua, USCF National Master, the University of Texas at Dallas, April, 2007.

Objectives: The students assess whether a bishop is better than a knight in given chess positions. Students cite an appropriate reason for the bishop's superiority. Furthermore, students suggest a move order that wins the game for the side with the good bishop.

Materials: Demonstration board. Figure 2.13 as homework or in-class assessment. If completing Figure 2.13 in class, pencils are needed. For teacher background (optional), read about the topics of good bishop versus bad knight (and good knight versus bad bishop) in Wolff (2005, pp. 182–183, 251–252) and Eade (2005, pp. 47, 188, 238–240, 241–242).

Procedure: Before class begins, set up the demonstration board with a position where the bishop is clearly superior to the knight, such as Figure 2.14. When class begins,

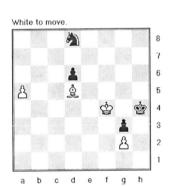

White to move.

The black N has no safe moves.

Figure 2.14.

1. Have the students sit where they can see the demonstration board.
2. Ask the students the point value of the bishop and the knight.
3. Once they say that each are worth three points ask, "But couldn't one be more powerful than the other in certain positions?"
4. Write on the blackboard or dry-erase board, "A bishop is better than an opposing knight when (A) the bishop limits the knight, now or in the near future, or (B) the bishop attacks the enemy pawns, now or in the near future, or (C) the position is open, making the bishop better than the knight."
5. Now direct the students' attention to Figure 2.14 on the demonstration board. Tell them "In this activity we will learn that even though bishops and knights are considered equal in points, sometimes the bishop can be stronger than a knight." Ask them for which reason is it better: A, B, or C. In Figure 2.14, answer A is correct. Show the winning strategy for Figure 2.14, which is to simply push white's passed a-pawn to its promotion square. This strategy is possible because the bishop is much better than the knight. In fact, the bishop attacks all the squares to which the knight might move. Ask the children questions about Figure 2.14 while showing it to them. For example, is the bishop a long-range piece, capable of covering many squares? What is the effect of that coverage, sometimes, on an opposing knight? Answers: The bishop is a long-range piece and can, at times, limit the knight's movements.

White to move

Bishop attacks the enemy pawns.

Figure 2.15.

White to move

Bishop is better in an open position.

Figure 2.16.

6. Now, show them another example. Figure 2.15 is particularly compelling. Ask the students why the bishop is better, as you point to the A, B, and C reasons written on the dry-erase board. The correct answer is B. White can win this position in 2 ways: Play **1. Bb3** followed by **2. Bg8** when the black pawns will fall. Or play **1. Bxf5** with a tactical breakthrough, for instance, after **1....gxf5** white plays **2. g6 hxg6.** Then white wins with **3. h7,** as the pawn will promote next move.

7. Construct Figure 2.16 on the demonstration board. Again, ask why the bishop is better than the knight: A, B, or C. In this case, answer C is the best answer. Answer B is also possible, since the bishop will attack the a6 pawn soon. Nevertheless, the most important factor in Figure 2.16 is the speed of a bishop on an open board. In Figure 2.16 the bishop will move from h1 to b7, attacking and then winning the enemy pawn on a6. In contrast, the knight takes several moves to reach the critical a-pawns. After Bxa6, white will move his bishop off the a-file and promote his pawn.

Evaluation: Hand out Figure 2.13, for completion in class or as homework. Answers to Figure 2.13 are in Appendix B.

♟ Stalemate Surprise

Objectives: Students use scientific inquiry to determine whether a pawn one square from promoting, adjacent to its own king, can hold a draw against an opponent's king and queen. Students record and compare results. Students recognize that the pawn is the independent variable in this chess experiment. Students learn that chess mistakes may be termed experimental error.

Materials: Demonstration board, set and board for every two students, two copies per student of Figure 1.6 (the score sheet), pencils. On the dry-erase board, create a chart with a column for each pawn (a-, b-, c-, d-, e-, f-, g-, and h-). For teacher background (optional), read about K & Q vs. K & P positions in Fine (1941, pp. 522–524).

Procedure: Assign students partners. Each pair sets up a white Kc6 and white Qe6. On the second rank set up a black pawn and a black king (on a file adjacent to the pawn). If more variety is desired, have some pairs instead set up a black Kc3 and a black Qe3, and a white pawn and white king on adjacent files on the seventh rank. Reversing the colors won't affect the nature of the position, but gives the students more cases to examine.

The pawn placement varies for each pair. That is, some pairs have an a-pawn, some have a b-pawn, and so forth (through h-pawn). Pairs play out their assigned position with the side with the queen making the first move. Each partner writes chess notation on a copy of Figure 1.6 as moves are made. The game continues until a result is reached (win, loss, or draw). Then each pair resets its initial position. The partner who had white before takes the black pieces the second time around. Once again, each partner writes notation on a copy of Figure 1.6. After the second time playing through the position, each pair discusses whether their particular set-up was a win, draw, or loss for the side with the pawn and why.

After pairs complete their private discussions, start a whole class discussion around the demonstration board. Pairs approach the demonstration board with their score sheets, so that they can show the class what moves they played when deciding whether their position was a win, loss, or draw for the defender. After each pair's report, write win, loss, or draw under the column for that pair's pawn (a-, b-, c-, d-, e-, f-, g-, and h-) on the dry-erase board.

After you have filled in the chart, students comprehend that the placement of the pawn was the independent variable in this experiment. They might also decide that the quality of the chess moves affected the experiment if, for example, one pair showed moves ending with a loss for the side with the K and Q. Discussion of experimental error is appropriate here. In science experiments there is always some degree of experimental error. When reporting their results, scientists estimate the effect of errors on data.

Have the students look for a pattern in the pairs' collected results that are recorded on the dry-erase board. Does the side with the pawn usually lose? Were pawns on particular files able to draw against the K & Q? Show the solution for each pawn (see Appendix B) on the demonstration board. The stalemate drawing solution might come as a surprise to some students. Comparison among the pairs' results and the official solutions should be made.

Evaluation: Grading may be based on how well the pairs worked together and on the whole class discussion. One measure of pair cooperation is the notation sheets that each partner filled out about their K & P vs. K & Q position. Another measure is your observation of each pair. The whole class discussion could be graded based on each pair's contribution to that discussion. The answers to the varying pawn placements are in Appendix B.

Chapter 3

MATHEMATICAL PROBLEM SOLVING

Connections to Math Standards

For the activities in this chapter, chess is the authentic context for problem solving using operations, fractions, decimals, percentages, measurement, probability, and geometry. According to the National Council of Teachers of Mathematics (NCTM), "For any assessment of problem solving, teachers must look beyond the answer to the reasoning behind the solution. This evidence can be found in written and oral explanations, drawings, and models" (2000, p. 187). By evaluating how students approach and solve these math and chess activities, educators "can choose directions for future instruction that fit with their mathematical goals" (NCTM, p. 187).

The first two activities in this chapter ("**Covering** the Board: Rooks" and "Covering the Board: Kings") share the theme of *domination* from graph theory, a part of geometry. I learned about the relationship of domination to chess from Watkins (2004). Watkins's domination introduction, quoted next, could be paraphrased for your students so that they understand the importance of covering activities.

The concept of domination is one of the central ideas in graph theory, and is especially important in the application of graph theory to the real world. Imagine a network of some kind, it could be a communication network such as a cellular phone system or perhaps a network of roads in your local community. Such systems often require vital transmission stations to make them work effectively. A cellular phone company must provide an adequate number of communication links suitably spaced so that customers always have a strong signal for their cell phones. Similarly, your local community needs to provide an adequate number of fire stations suitably spaced so that there is a satisfactory response time to fires anywhere within the community. And, of course, both the phone company and your city council need to do this in a way that is as economical as possible, which means building as few communication links or fire stations as possible. (Watkins, 2004, p. 95)

Not only are domination problems important for graph theory and real-world math applications, but they are critical for chess understanding. Chess pieces attack (dominate) all the squares to which they can move. In contrast, pawns attack **diagonal**ly but move forward. With the exception of the rook, all pieces attack fewer squares when placed in corners than when placed in the middle of the board. However, bishops, kings, and queens are proportionally less handicapped by corner placement than are knights. As shown in Figure 3.1, a knight can move to two squares from the corner of the board but can move to eight squares from the board's center. Therefore, it is said that a knight on the rim (edge of the board or the corner) is dim. Figure 3.2 shows a bishop's coverage from the corner and from the center.

Noted chess teacher and USCF senior master Fred Lindsay starts new students with domination concepts. That is, he demonstrates how placement affects the number of squares covered. Here's my account, Root (2006, October), of Lindsay's lesson with then 13-year-old novice Jeff Ashton, now a USCF chess master and the creator of *Black Box* in chapter 2:

The initial lesson was not what Jeff expected. There were no secret checkmates. Instead Fred put a piece in the middle of an empty board and asked Jeff to tell him how many squares it could move to. Then Fred put the same piece on the side, and had Jeff answer the same question. Jeff recalls, "We went through all the pieces, and I'll never forget the impact this first lesson had on my knowledge of preferred piece placement." (p. 27)

Ne5 attacks eight squares.

Na1 attacks two squares.

Figure 3.1.
A knight on the rim is dim.

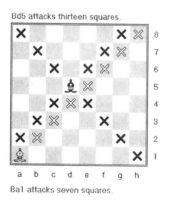

Bd5 attacks thirteen squares.

Ba1 attacks seven squares.

Figure 3.2.

Covering the Board: Rooks

Objectives: Students determine the minimum number of rooks that are needed to cover every square on an 8-by-8 board. Students describe the moves of the rook as vertical and horizontal. As an extension or homework, students extrapolate to boards of different dimensions and/or begin to learn how to checkmate with two rooks against a king.

Materials: Blank 8-by-8 chess diagrams, at least one per student. Nine colored pencils with erasers per student. Demonstration board.

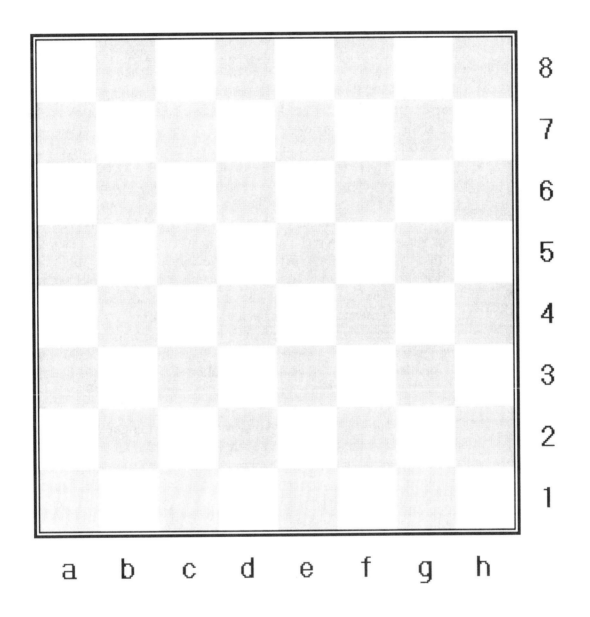

Figure 3.3.
8-by-8 board.

From *Science, Math, Checkmate: 32 Chess Activities for Inquiry and Problem Solving* by Alexey W. Root. Westport, CT: Teacher Ideas Press. Copyright © 2008.

Optional: copies of 7-by-7 and 9-by-9 chess diagrams. Set and board for every two students if planning to introduce *Checkmating with Two Rooks* (Root, 2006, pp. 64–65).

Procedure: Teach or review on the demonstration board the vertical and horizontal movements of the rook. Tell students that the abbreviation for the rook is R. Place a rook on a square of the board, for example Re4. Run your hand or a pointer up and down the e-file, noting that the R attacks and can move to any square on the e-file. Then show that the R also covers the fourth rank. Reposition the R on f6. Point to f7, asking the students to give thumbs up if the R attacks f7. Repeat with other squares on the f-file and sixth rank. The students should give the thumbs-up signal each time. To check their understanding, point to e7 and see if they correctly give you the thumbs-down signal because the R moves only horizontally and vertically, not diagonally. Move your hands vertically, horizontally, and diagonally as your students say those words and copy your gestures.

Challenge the students by stating, "On a board with no other pieces or pawns, a rook can reach any square in just two moves." Place the R on d3. Ask how the R can get to h8 in two moves. If the students' answer is R to d4 to h8, then the students mistakenly think that rooks can move diagonally. The two correct answers are Rd3-h3-h8 or Rd3-d8-h8.

Remind or teach the students that the R attacks every square to which it can move, as shown in Figure 3.6. Note that both the white R on a1 and the black R on b2 cover a2 and b1. Place the R on different squares on the board and ask the students to count how many squares that the R covers. (Answer: From any square on an open board, the R can move to 14 squares.)

Tell students that their individual assignment is to figure out how many rooks are needed to cover every square on the board. Students should represent each rook that they place on the board with a different-colored "R" and mark the squares covered by that R in the same color. In Figure 3.6, for example, if a blue pencil was used to write "R" on a1, the blue pencil should also be used to mark every square along the a-file and along the first rank.

Walk around the room as students work on their individual assignments. As students will complete coloring in Figure 3.3 at different rates, you might have Figure 3.4 and Figure 3.5 available. Or you might introduce, to small groups who have finished coloring, the lesson plan *Checkmating with Two Rooks.*

Evaluation: As students are coloring their chess diagrams (Figure 3.3), determine whether individual students understand the moves of the rook by asking them to show you, with finger movements on their chess diagrams, the squares that the R attacks. See whether their diagrams include eight rooks to cover all the squares. Figure 3.7 uses just seven rooks; thus the square h8 is not covered by any rook.

As a homework or extension activity, ask students how many rooks are needed for a square board with side *n* (number). If *n* is too abstract,

Figure 3.4.
7-by-7 board.

Figure 3.5.
9-by-9 board.

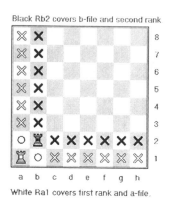

Figure 3.6.
Rook moves.

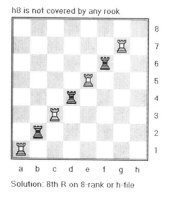

Figure 3.7.

ask them about 7-by-7 or 9-by-9 boards. Pass out the 7-by-7 and 9-by-9 boards to take home or to work on as an extension in class. The answer is that *n* rooks are needed to cover a square board of size *n* by *n*.

Perimeter and Surface Area of the Board

This activity is an edited version of a lesson plan written by Anna Katzman, the University of Texas at Dallas, April, 2007.

Objectives: Students apply prior knowledge of perimeter and surface area formulas to measure a board. Specifically, the students find the perimeter and the surface area of the board by using one square as a unit. The students either turn in their calculations or summarize and present their findings in class.

Materials: Copies of Figure 3.3 (one copy for every two students), dry-erase board, and pencils.

Procedure: Tell the class to calculate the perimeter and the surface area of the board by using one square as one unit. Assign each student a partner, and ask each pair to have out a pencil. Pass out copies of Figure 3.3 to each pair of students. Write the following two questions on the dry-erase board, asking students not to call out the answers:

1. What is the perimeter of the board?
2. What is the surface area of the board?

Ask the students to write the solutions for these two questions on the bottom of Figure 3.3, showing their work either by writing the formula or by using words to explain their procedure.

Evaluation: Collect the copies of Figure 3.3 from each pair or ask pairs of students to present their findings in class and explain their solutions. At the end of the presentations, or after Figure 3.3 papers have been collected, ask, "How does finding the perimeter differ from finding the surface area of a figure?" Listen to students' answers and provide feedback. Finally, check students' papers or presentations for the correct answers, given in Appendix B.

Covering the Board: Kings

Objectives: Students determine how many kings are needed to cover every square on the 8-by-8 board. Students additionally prove through use of diagrams and logic that the same number of kings covers a 7-by-7 board or a 9-by-9 board.

Materials: Blank chess diagrams of sizes 7-by-7 (Figure 3.4), 8-by-8 (Figure 3.3), and 9-by-9 (Figure 3.5). Each student receives one copy of either Figure 3.4, or Figure 3.3, or Figure 3.5. Demonstration board,

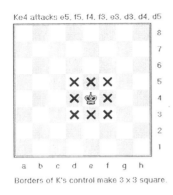

Ke4 attacks e5, f5, f4, f3, e3, d3, d4, d5

Borders of K's control make 3 x 3 square.

Figure 3.8.
King moves.

pencils, large post-it notes (big enough to cover one square of the demonstration board); mark each post-it note with an "X." Dry-erase board.

Procedure: Teach or review the movements of the king, noting that the abbreviation for king is K. State, "The king moves one square in any direction, vertically, horizontally, or diagonally. The squares the king can move to are the same squares that the king attacks." Place the K on e4 on the demonstration board. Point to e5 and ask the students to give you the thumbs-up signal if the K covers e5. The response should be thumbs up. Repeat the thumbs-up routine with other squares adjacent to the K, marking those squares with the large post-it notes to show K's coverage. For variety, occasionally point to a square outside the K's range such as d7 or h1 so that students give you the thumbs-down sign. Ask the students the shape of the borders of the king's coverage. They should respond that the borders form a 3-by-3 square.

Ask students to think to themselves about square boards of different sizes, such as 7-by-7, 8-by-8, and 9-by-9. As you are passing out the paper chess diagrams, ask them to silently speculate about how many 3-by-3 squares cover boards of different dimensions.

Each student should have one paper chess diagram, of size 7-by-7, or 8-by-8, or 9-by-9. Instruct students that they should place capital letter Ks on the board such that every square on the board is covered by a king and that the minimum number of kings is used to complete the domination task.

After students have worked for five minutes, have students combine in mixed groups so that each group has students holding 7-by-7, 8-by-8, and 9-by-9 board diagrams. Ask each mixed group to answer the following questions in writing on the back of Figure 3.4, 3.3, or 3.5. Write the questions on the dry-erase board as you say them aloud:

1. How many Ks are needed to dominate every square on the 7-by-7, 8-by-8, and 9-by-9 boards?
2. Explain your answer for number 1 by drawing diagrams, using words, or writing a mathematical expression.

Evaluation: The groups should arrive at the following answers. (1) Nine kings are needed to dominate boards of sizes 7-by-7, 8-by-8, and 9-by-9. (2) Watkins (2004, pp. 102–103) gives chess diagram illustrations and mathematical equations of the solution set. Figure 3.9 shows the "nine highlighted squares that must be covered on each chessboard" (p. 103). As Watkins explains, "No matter where we might place a king on any of these boards, it will cover only one of these highlighted squares; in other words, a king can't ever cover two of the highlighted squares at the same time" (p. 102). Consider whether your students' solutions exhibit similar logic and arrive at the correct answer.

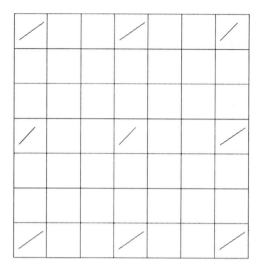

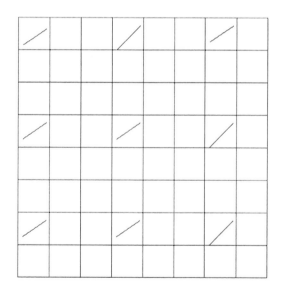

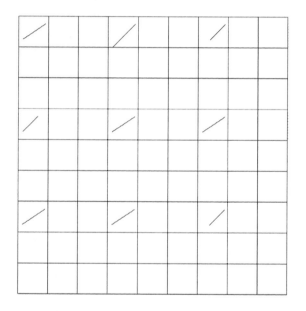

Figure 3.9.
The / marks highlight the nine squares on each board that must be covered.

According to Watkins (2004), "the concept of independence is closely related to that of domination, and is, in its own right, one of the central ideas in graph theory" (p. 163). The independence concept inspired the next activity in this chapter, "Eight Queens."

♟ Eight Queens

Objective: Students determine how to place eight queens on the board so that none of the queens attacks any other queen. Alternatively, students place as many queens on the board as they can without any queen attacking another queen.

Materials: Boards for every two students, with eight chess-queen substitutes for every board. Since you are not likely to have so many queens for each board, tell the students to use pawns as stand-ins for queens. One copy of Figure 3.3 (the 8-by-8 board) and one pencil for every two students. Demonstration board. Polgar (2006, p. 15) and Khmelnitsky, Khodarkovsky, and Zadorozny (2006, Book 2, p. 154) recommend using the eight-queens problem as a lesson for beginning chess students. Watkins (2004) gives theoretical background for the problem.

Procedure: Teach or review how the queen moves, noting the Q abbreviation for the queen. State, "The queen combines the moves of the rook and the bishop. On any given move, she can choose to move like a rook (vertically or horizontally) or like a bishop (diagonally)." Place the queen on the demonstration board, and have the students signal thumbs up when you make legal queen moves and thumbs down when you make illegal queen moves. If the move is a legal move, you might additionally call on a student to say if that queen's move was vertical, horizontal, or diagonal. Tell students that the queen attacks the same squares to which she can move. In Figure 3.10, the white queen (Q) on g7 attacks the black knight (N) on g1 because she can move to that square.

The eight-queens problem is to place eight queens on an 8-by-8 board so that none of the queens attacks any other queen. This problem is difficult. Therefore, an alternative challenge is for students to place as many queens on the board as they can without any of them attacking each other. Give the history of the eight-queens chess problem (Watkins, 2004, pp. 164–165). The problem first appeared in a German chess newspaper in 1848. It was found to have 92 solutions if the eight queens are considered identical. Many of those 92 solutions are rotations and reflections.

Pair up students to find a solution to the eight-queens problem, as shown in Figure 3.11. If any pair of students finds an eight-queens solution, have them record it on Figure 3.3 by writing Q on each square where they've placed a queen. If there are multiple eight-queen solutions generated by the class, collect the papers and post them on a bulletin

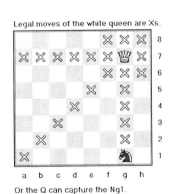

Legal moves of the white queen are Xs.

Or the Q can capture the Ng1.

Figure 3.10.
A queen's moves and captures.

Figure 3.11.
Solving the eight-queens problem.

board. Label the first paper posted as "Solution 1," the second paper posted as "Solution 2," and so forth. For an extension, have students figure out which of the posted solutions are rotations and reflections of other posted solutions, and which ones are unique solutions.

It is possible that no pair of students will find a solution to the eight-queens problem during the class period. You can back-track to the alternate objective. Or you can decide whether to give the eight-queens problem as homework, sending home blank diagrams (copies of Figure 3.3) with the students.

Evaluation: Be sure to praise students who successfully placed seven queens. Remind students that placing eight queens has been considered a worthy challenge for 160 years. If a pair of students claims a solution, check to see if the students placed the eight queens so that none of the queens attacked any other queen. Also determine if the students correctly transferred their solutions onto diagrams (copies of Figure 3.3), using a Q to designate each queen's location. If the class completed the extension activity, were students able to notice solutions that were reflections and rotations? Appendix B gives one solution to the eight-queens problem.

♟ Balancing Chess Equations

Objective: Students cooperatively form balanced equations, using operations, with chess pieces of predetermined values.

Materials: One set of 30 chess pawns and pieces (leave out the two kings), four "equation stations" (desks) equipped with paper, pencils, reward stickers, one copy per station of the = symbol, and two copies per station of +, –, x, and / symbols. Dry-erase board.

Procedure: Write the following abbreviations and values on the dry-erase board: Pawn = P, Knight = N, Bishop = B, Rook = R, Queen = Q, King = K. The values of the pawns and pieces are: ♟ (P) = 1, ♞ (N) = 3, ♝ (B) = 3, ♜ (R) = 5, ♛ (Q) = 9, and the ♚ (K) is not used for this exercise. The king is invaluable because if he is checkmated the game is lost. The values of the other pawns and pieces are based on their mobility in a chess game.

Explain that one to three students will be on each side of an equation station. To succeed at the station, the sides of the equation must balance. If balance is achieved, everyone at the station gets a reward sticker. The activity ends when, according to your observations, each student has attempted to make an equation with every other student.

Give a demonstration with you (the teacher) at an equation station. Four students, holding a P, B, N, and Q respectively, approach your equation station. How can the students arrange themselves on each side of the desk to make a balanced equation? The class shares ideas to arrive at this solution: Q/P = BxN or, in numbers, 9/1 = 3x3. The teacher, modeling the task of the equation station personnel, should write up the balanced equation first with chess abbreviations and then with numbers. Because the group came up with an equation, keep one sticker for yourself and pass out one sticker to each of the four students.

Optional hints to share with students: Equations that use the commutative property of addition 3+5 = 5+3 are the easiest to form. Some sets of pieces, for example P, R, Q, and Q, cannot be arranged in an equation.

Students are now ready to try this as a class. Distribute the chess pawns and pieces to students by asking review questions. While temporarily hiding the piece values on the dry-erase board, ask "What piece is worth five points?" The student that answers "rook" gets handed the rook to hold. Stop distributing when four students remain without pawns or pieces. Those four students become equation station monitors.

Students holding a pawn or a piece approach equation stations in groups of three to six students, discuss possible equations, and arrange themselves/their pieces into an equation. As soon as he or she records that particular equation, the equation station monitor gives stickers to himself (or herself) and to the chess-figure holding students. Then those students should disband and regroup with new students at another equation station.

Evaluation: Monitor the activity to see if students are cooperatively working to find solutions. After the activity is over, examine the papers collected from each equation station, looking for the following: Are chess piece and pawn values correct? Are numbers and math operation symbols used correctly? Do the equations balance?

♟ Pawns, Pieces, Proportions, and Probability

Objectives: Students understand fractions as parts of wholes. In particular, students will recognize what fractions of the total chess army are comprised by the pawns and by the different types of pieces. Students convert fractions to decimals and percentages. Students record their selections of chess pieces and pawns from bagged sets.

Materials: Sets, photocopies for each group of Figures 3.12 and 3.13, scratch paper, bags (or boxes) to hold sets, blindfolds (optional), pencils.

Procedure: Introduce the six types of chess figures: pawn, knight, bishop, rook, queen, and king. Once the students can identify the piece or pawn displayed, assign them one of two procedures for determining the likelihood of selecting a particular type of piece or a pawn out of a bagged set. Half the class will record on Figure 3.12 their 32 attempts at selecting pieces and pawns from a bagged set. Figure 3.14 shows a blindfolded student drawing a queen out of a bagged set. The other half

Names _____

DATA FORM

For the 32 trials, students in your group take turns drawing out one piece or pawn at a time from the set in the bag. The person selecting closes his or her eyes or wears a blindfold. Take turns recording the results of each trial, writing in the second column P (pawn), N (knight), B (bishop), R (rook), Q (queen), or K (king) depending on which chess figure was pulled out of the bag. Disregard the color of the chess figure; just record its type (abbreviation). Put each figure back in the bag after it is recorded for that trial. In the analysis of data (column 3), work together to answer the questions listed.

Column 1	Column 2	Column 3
Trial #	Which piece or pawn?	Analysis
1 2 3 4 5 6 7 8 9 10 11 12 13		After collecting data in the first two columns of the table, answer the following questions. Express your answers in the form of a reduced fraction. For example, if a pawn was selected 14 of 32 times, that is 14/32 which reduces to 7/16. How often was a pawn selected?_____ How often was a knight selected?_____ How often was a bishop selected?_____ How often was a rook selected?_____ How often was a queen selected?_____ How often was a king selected?_____

14		
15		
16		
17		
18		
19		
20		
21		
22		
23		
24		
25		
26		
27		
28		
29		
30		
31		
32		

Figure 3.12.
Data form.

Names _____

PROPORTION FORM

For this form, you and your group members write answers for the questions in each column. The P (pawn) answer is done for you as a model. Everyone in the group individually calculates each answer on scratch paper. Then one group member writes the answer preferred by the group on this form. To check column 4 answers, add all the proportions in the fourth column. The correct total is 32/32. 32/32 reduces to 1, which represents the one complete set of chess pieces. Can you check your work in a similar way for the fractions in column 5? What about for the decimals and percentages in column 6?

Column 1 Chess figure? (P, N, B, R, Q, or K)	Column 2 How many of this figure in one chess set?	Column 3 Total number of pawns & pieces in a set?	Column 4 Proportion of figure/total number?	Column 5 Reduce the fraction to its simplest form.	Column 6 Extra credit: express the fraction as a decimal or a percent.
P	16	32	16/32	1/2	.5 or 50%
		32			
		32			
		32			
		32			
		32			
		32			
		32			

Figure 3.13.
Proportion form.

From *Science, Math, Checkmate: 32 Chess Activities for Inquiry and Problem Solving* by Alexey W. Root. Westport, CT: Teacher Ideas Press. Copyright © 2008.

Figure 3.14.
Blindfolded student selects piece from bag.

calculates the mathematical proportions of pawns and pieces in a set on scratch paper before recording their answers on Figure 3.13. Groups within each half of the class can be as small as two or as big as four. Then the halves switch tasks. At the end of class, results will be discussed. Was there a bias when drawing out pieces and pawns, because larger pieces were more easily grabbed? How close did the drawing-out data correspond to the mathematical model?

Evaluation: During the activity, see if students are on task and participating. During the discussion, call on volunteers to answer this question from Figure 3.13, "Can you check your work for the fractions in column 5 and the decimals and percentages in column 6 in a similar way to the checking process for column 4? Explain your answer." Each volunteer may have a different way of explaining his or her answer, but the answer should be "yes." All parts of the set, taken together, make a whole: Fractions add up to 1, decimals add up to 1, and percentages combined equal 100%. To check the problem-solving process behind the Figure 3.13, ask students to turn in their scratch paper calculations. Groups also submit Figure 3.12 and Figure 3.13 for assessment.

♟ Practice Producing Polygons

Objectives: Students connect coordinate geometry and the algebraic notation system for naming the squares of the board. Students review the names, shapes, and properties of polygons.

Materials: Overhead transparency or dry-erase board representation of the x- and y-axes of the Cartesian plane, quadrant I. Demonstration board. Class set of Figure 3.15, pencils. Optional: Figure 2.10 for teacher reference if you want to teach chess-diagram making during this lesson.

Procedure: Draw the first quadrant of the Cartesian plane on the dry-erase board or overhead projector. Your drawing should look like Figure 3.16. Review the x- and y-axes and call on students to identify points of the form (x, y). Point out similarities and differences between the quadrant and the board. Some similarities: The plane and the board both use coordinates. On the first quadrant of the plane, one finds a given location by first moving horizontally left-to-right along the x-axis and then moving vertically from bottom-to-top along the y-axis. On the board, one first finds the file by moving left-to-right horizontally and then one finds the rank location vertically from bottom-to-top. Some differences: In the case of the board, however, the coordinates refer to entire squares

Name _____

POLYGONS

Use Xs in the middle of chessboard squares to show the perimeters of three polygons on the chess diagrams. Then list the properties specific to each polygon. All polygons are closed-sided figures with only straight sides. An example of properties of a specific polygon: A square has four congruent sides, four right angles, and two sets of parallel sides. You might outline the borders any of the following: quadrilateral, square, triangle, trapezoid, parallelogram, hexagon, pentagon, octagon, decagon, rectangle, and rhombus (diamond). Tell the specific properties of each polygon that you draw.

Use Xs to mark the perimeter of polygon

```
                              8
                              7
                              6
                              5
                              4
                              3
                              2
                              1
   a   b   c   d   e   f   g   h
```

What polygon did you draw?_____What are the properties specific to this

polygon?_____

Use Xs to mark the perimeter of polygon

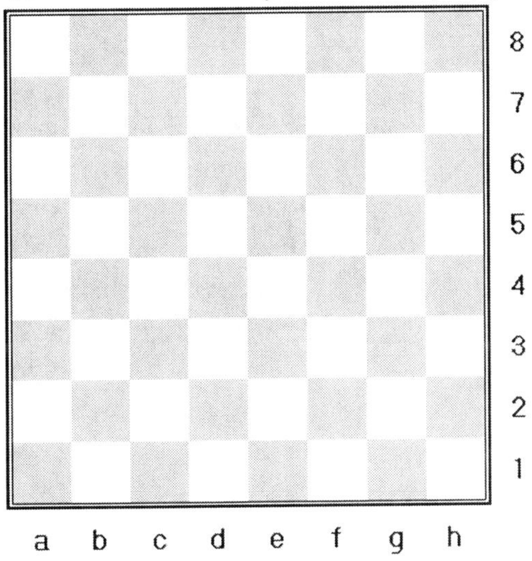

								8
								7
								6
								5
								4
								3
								2
								1

a b c d e f g h

What polygon did you draw?_____What are the properties specific to this

polygon?_____

Use Xs to mark the perimeter of polygon

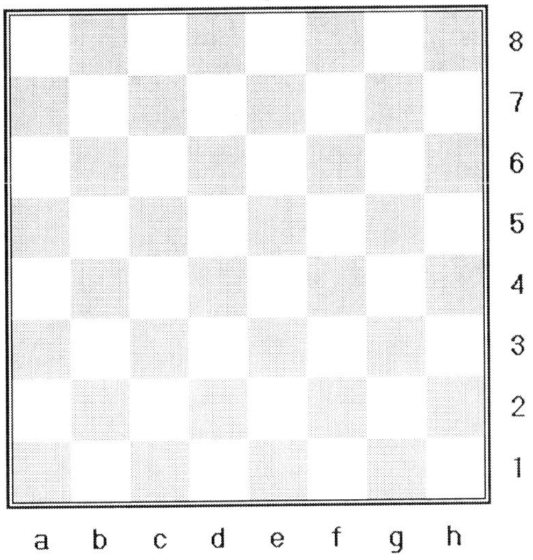

								8
								7
								6
								5
								4
								3
								2
								1

a b c d e f g h

What polygon did you draw?_____What are the properties specific to this

polygon?_____

Figure 3.15.
Polygons.

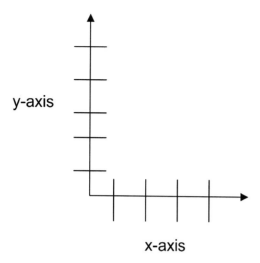

Figure 3.16.
Cartesian Plane, Quadrant I.

What shape is made?

What are the properties of this shape?

Figure 3.17.
Square.

rather than to points. The coordinate plane employs numbers on both its x- and y-axes. The board uses lower-case letters along its x-axis, and numbers along its y-axis.

As you call students to the chess demonstration board, hand each one a piece or pawn to place on a square whose coordinates you name. For example, when Susie approaches the demonstration board hand her a white pawn. Tell her to place the pawn on e4, while saying to the rest of the class, "Susie put the white pawn on e4." In this way, students hear the piece and pawn names while also learning the notation of the squares.

After Susie has placed her pawn, ask other students to put a pawn or piece on the demonstration board. Say, for example, "Put a white pawn on c3, a white knight on e3, a black bishop on c5, a white pawn on e5, a black queen on d5, a white pawn on e4, a white bishop on d3, and a white king on c4." As the students place pawns and pieces on the demonstration board, a shape is formed. The students watching should raise their hands once they recognize that the shape is a square. Review the properties of a square.

If you would prefer the students use piece and pawn abbreviations rather than Xs to mark the borders of polygons in Figure 3.15, teach how to make a chess diagram (using Figure 2.10 as your reference). Then pass out Figure 3.15, one copy per student. Before students begin their individual worksheets, announce whether they may assist each other. If helping is allowed, students will likely communicate mathematically about the definitions of polygons. When students have completed Figure 3.15, invite a student to the front of the class to call out a shape from it. Replacing the Figure 3.15 Xs with pawns and pieces, as the teacher modeled earlier in this activity, the student directs several classmates to make one of his or her Figure 3.15 polygons on the demonstration board. The rest of the class should guess which polygon is being formed. Once a guess is correct, the student completes the polygon (if any parts are still missing) and tells the properties of that polygon.

Evaluation: During class, pay attention to how fast the class guesses a polygon as it takes shape on the demonstration board. Listen to each student's description of the properties of his or her polygon. Have all students turn in Figure 3.15 for assessment.

The next activity, Chess Players' Stats, came from an experience that my son William and I had at the 2006 U.S. Open chess tournament. The nine-round tournament had just ended, and we were standing with a small crowd of people at the tournament's **wall chart.** We saw that the

U.S. Open winner, Grandmaster Yury Shulman, scored eight out of nine points. William, who was nine years old at the time, quickly estimated Yury's winning percentage. Then two other tournament players asked William what their scores were in percentages!

♟ Chess Players' Stats

Objectives: Given a chess tournament of X number of rounds, students will estimate or calculate the percentage scored by particular players in the event. Students interpret data from a chess tournament **crosstable.**

Materials: Print out a crosstable from a chess tournament or use Figure 3.18. To find other crosstables, go to the USCF homepage http://www.uschess.org. Select "Clubs & Tourneys" and then "Past Event Crosstables." Or, from the homepage, click on "Players & Ratings," and then on "Player/Rating Lookup." Look up the name of a USCF member such as "Shulman, Yury." To continue our example, once you are on GM Shulman's member page, click on "Tnmt. Hst." which stands for Tournament History. For August 13, 2006, you find the crosstable for the U.S. Open.

Photocopy a class set of Figure 3.18. Optional: Calculators for calculating percentages. For example 5/9 is .56% (rounded), a calculation easier to do by calculator than by hand. Students need pencils too.

Procedure: Depending on how comfortable your class is with percentages, you may choose to start the class with a review of how to convert fractions to percentages. Ask students to estimate whether 5/9 is closer to 25% or 50%, and then to explain their reasoning. Then ask some other fraction to percentage estimation questions: Is 2/11 closer to 20% or 40%? Is 3/8 closer to 15% or 50%? Ask students to explain how they decided.

Pass out Figure 3.18 to students, keeping a copy for you. Ask some questions to check for students' comprehension of the crosstable. For example, who did Yury play in round one? (Answer: A player with **pairing** number 147. The tournament had 543 players; only a portion of the crosstable is reproduced here.) What was the result for Yury of that round one game? (Answer: Yury won. W means win.) How did Alfonso Almeida (pairing number 10) do in his game against Yury? (Answer: He lost to Yury in round seven.)

When the students seem to understand the crosstable, allow them to work individually on the questions. Encourage them to use a variety of methods for questions 2 (estimation) and 3 (calculating). Ask them to show their work on Figure 3.18, or on the back if they need additional room.

Evaluation: Either grade the worksheet later or review the answers and the students' problem-solving methods in class. At this point, I share William's method for estimating. William knew that the U.S. Open tournament had nine rounds, and that 9 x 11 = 99, which is close to 100.

2006 U.S. Open crosstable

Pair #	Player Name	Total Points	Rd. 1	Rd. 2	Rd. 3	Rd. 4	Rd. 5	Rd. 6	Rd. 7	Rd. 8	Rd. 9
1	Yury Shulman	8.0	W147	W85	W58	W54	W13	D6	W10	W4	D7
2	Zviad Izoria	7.5	W269	W136	W370	W20	W11	D5	D7	D25	W24
3	Gregory Kaidanov	7.5	W249	W92	W64	W34	D8	W24	L6	W35	W27
4	Alexander Shabalov	7.5	W149	W43	W37	W28	D7	W46	W5	L1	W25
5	Giorgi Kacheishvili	7.5	W257	W172	W76	W56	W32	D2	L4	W34	W28
6	Joel Benjamin	7.5	W205	W123	W77	W107	W40	D1	W3	L7	W29
7	Emilio Cordova	7.5	W295	W117	W66	W61	D4	W31	D2	W6	D1
8	Dmitry Gurevich	7.5	W209	W130	W226	W60	D3	D29	D17	W51	W30
9	John Fedorowicz	7.5	W336	W238	D53	W84	W48	D19	W103	W17	D11
10	Alfonso Almeida	7.5	W312	W163	W115	D19	W39	W155	L1	W107	W33
11	Michael Aigner	7.5	W261	W127	W122	W227	L2	W42	W192	W16	D9
12	Florin Felecan	7.0	W206	W95	W79	L32	W115	D38	W44	D59	W57

Abbreviations: Pair # = Pairing Number; Rd. = Round; W = Win, D = Draw, L = Loss; W147 = the player had a win against the player with pairing number 147. This is only a portion of the crosstable, so the name of player 147, Jennifer Skidmore, is not shown above.

For parts b and c of 2 and 3 below, show your work here or on the back of the paper:

1. In what round did Joel Benjamin (pairing # 6) draw against Yury Shulman?_____

2a. How many points did Florin Felecan (pairing # 12) score in the tournament? _____

2b. Estimate what percentage Felecan scored:

2c. Calculate Felecan's actual percentage:

3a. How many points did Yury Shulman score in the tournament?

3b. Estimate what percentage Shulman scored:

3c. Calculate Shulman's actual percentage:

Figure 3.18.
U.S. Open crosstable worksheet.

From *Science, Math, Checkmate: 32 Chess Activities for Inquiry and Problem Solving* by Alexey W. Root. Westport, CT: Teacher Ideas Press. Copyright © 2008.

Therefore, to estimate a player's percentage, he multiplied the points they scored by 11. William noted that his method would work for tournaments with any number of rounds. For example, for a six-round tournament, each point scored would be multiplied by 17 because 6 x 17 = 102. A score of two points in a six-round tournament would be approximately 34%. The answers for Figure 3.18 are in Appendix B.

♟ Pick a Pocketful of Pieces

Objectives: Students determine the probability of a particular compound event. Students communicate mathematically with each other to solve a probability problem.

Materials: Scratch paper, pencils, chess pieces, value of chess pieces written on the dry-erase board. The values of the pawns and pieces are: ♙ (pawn/P) = 1, ♘ (knight/N) = 3, ♗ (bishop/B) = 3, ♖ (rook/R) = 5, ♕ (queen/Q) = 9, and the ♔ (king/K) is not used for this activity.

Procedure: Tell students that you have five chess figures in your pocket: one pawn, one knight, one bishop, one rook, and one queen. Reach into your pocket and pull out three chess figures, one at a time or in a handful of three. After all three figures have been chosen, have students add the values of the figures. Then place those three figures back in your pocket. Repeat this procedure two or three times. Then ask the students to predict the chance that the combined value of the three figures that you select will be seven. First encourage the students to figure out that only a B, N, and P added together make seven. Then ask the students how likely it is that you will draw out figures worth exactly seven points the next time you reach into your pocket for three figures. Record their guesses in percentages. Some students might say it is 25% likely that reaching in your pocket will yield a B, N, and P combination, others may guess higher or lower.

Tell students that they can figure out the probability for the seven-point combination, or for any other combination of chess figures. Some methods for solving this problem include making a tree diagram, constructing a chart, or multiplying fractions or decimals. (Wait to try this activity until students know one or all of these methods.) Have students work in small groups of two to four on the problem. Circulate to assess how the mathematical communication and problem solving is progressing. Invite several of the groups to present their solutions to the class.

Evaluation: Assess students' group work and their presentations. Two approaches to the solution are shown in Appendix B.

The next activity, Mazes and Monsters, asks students to find efficient routes or networks for pieces to capture stationary pawns and pieces. This chess activity incorporates visualization, spatial reasoning, and geometric modeling. As such, it fits into the standards for grades 6 through 8.

Students can also benefit from experience with other visual models, such as networks, to use in analyzing and solving real problems, such as those concerned with efficiency. . . . Such an investigation in the middle grades is a precursor of later work with Euler circuits, a foundation for work with sophisticated networks. (NCTM, 2000, pp. 237–238)

♞Mazes and Monsters

Objective: Students use a monster piece to capture maze-arranged pawns and pieces of the opposite color.

Materials: Class set of Figure 3.19, demonstration board. Sets and boards, one for each pair of students. Pencils, one per student. Nottingham, Wade, and Lawrence (1998, p. 40) wrote that chess maze exercises "are good practice for thinking moves out ahead in a real game." Polgar (2006) includes mazes in her curricula. MacEnulty (2006) describes chess mazes from the point of view of the attacking piece, which is truly a monster. Pandolfini (1995, p. 159) credits Bruce Albertson with the creation of the monster chess teaching technique.

Procedure: Arrange the Bishop Maze from Figure 3.19 on the demonstration board. Explain that the black pawns and pieces cannot move. Instead, they form a maze for the white piece to traverse. The white piece, in contrast to the black ones, is a monster. The monster moves constantly, taking everything in its path. For example, white's bishop takes all 11 of black's pieces and pawns, capturing one piece or pawn per move. Ask students for the first couple of moves in the maze solution, and write those moves on the dry-erase board.

If students seem to understand how to continue, pass out Figure 3.19. Have students copy the first couple of moves from the dry-erase board onto their Figure 3.19 worksheet. Allow the students to complete the worksheet on their own. They may set up each maze with a board and set, but many will choose to solve the mazes using a pencil and Figure 3.19. As they finish Figure 3.19, have them pair up with boards and sets to make mazes for each other—with the monster piece being the K, N, B, R, or Q. If the maze is set up correctly, then the designated monster piece can make a capture on each move. Checks are ignored, since the "maze" pieces and pawns can't move.

Evaluation: Two of the possible solutions for Figure 3.19 are in the answer key in Appendix B. Walk around the room as students set up mazes for each other. See if the student-created mazes are solvable by monster pieces.

♗ Working Backward

Objectives: Students work backward from a checkmate to discover the preceding two moves, which have a pattern. Then students make multiple moves that follow the same checkmating pattern, given the same

BISHOP MAZE AND ROOK MAZE

For each maze, write the algebraic notation for the captures made by the monster piece (white bishop in the first maze, white rook in the second maze). Remember that a capture must be made on each move, and that every black piece and pawn must be captured. The black pieces and pawns cannot move in either maze.

White bishop is a monster piece.

Write the notation of white's captures: _____

White rook is a monster piece.

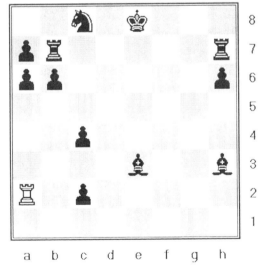

Write the notation of white's captures: _____

Figure 3.19.
Bishop and rook mazes.

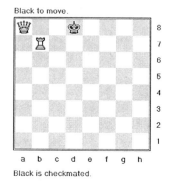

Black to move.

Black is checkmated.

Figure 3.20.
Checkmate!

White to move.

White to checkmate in one move.

Figure 3.21.

Black to move.

Black king is in check from R on b7.

Figure 3.22.

pieces (arranged differently). Optional: Compare to a math problem that uses a working backward strategy.

Materials: Demonstration board. For teacher background (optional), see Khmelnitsky, Khodarkovsky, and Zadorozny (2006, Book 1, pp. 113–118). Pandolfini (1995, p. 206) calls a teaching method similar to working backward **redactive instruction.**

Procedure: Show the position in Figure 3.20 on the demonstration board. Ask students, "Has white just moved the rook or the queen?" The answer must be the queen, since black could not legally have been in check before the white queen mated. Therefore, the position immediately before Figure 3.20 could not have had a queen on the eighth rank. The queen could have come from several squares to get to a8, but one possibility (a6) is shown in Figure 3.21. Show the position in Figure 3.21 on the demonstration board. Call on a student to solve the mate in one, 1. Qa8#, which repeats Figure 3.20. Then set up Figure 3.22 on the demonstration board. The black king is in check from the white rook on b7. Ask students, "Has white just moved the rook or the queen?" Since the rook is checking the king, the rook has just moved into that position, perhaps from b5. Show another position on the demonstration board, Figure 3.23. Ask students to figure out how white can mate black in two moves. Compliment students when they answer 1. Rb7+ Kd8 (or e8 or f8) 2. Qa8#. Remind students that they've seen this checkmate before, as Figure 3.20 at the beginning of class. Ask students to describe the pattern of rook check–queen check, and how each of white's moves drives the black king back one more row. Back up the position another two moves, so that the R is on b3, the Q on a4, and the black king on the fifth rank. Ask students to find the four-move mate: 1. Rb5+ K to sixth rank 2. Qa6+ K to seventh rank 3. Rb7+ K to eighth rank 4. Qa8#. To avoid capture of the rook, be sure it is either more than one square away from the enemy king or that it is protected by its queen. That is, the enemy king cannot take the rook if such a capture would put it in check by the queen.

Set up Figure 3.24 on the demonstration board. Tell students that the position is white to move and mate in six moves. Remind students of the pattern of rook check–queen check, and advise them to repeat that pattern three times. Call on a student to tell the moves of the checkmate: 1. Rb3+ K to fourth rank 2. Qa4+ K to fifth rank 3. Rb5+ K to sixth rank 4. Qa6+ K to seventh rank 5. Rb7+ K to eighth rank 6. Qa8#.

White to move.

White can checkmate in two moves.

Figure 3.23.

White to move.

White can checkmate in six moves.

Figure 3.24.

Pair up students and pass out sets and boards. Ask pairs of students to set up a position with the black (defending) K on e5, the white R on h1, and the white Q on d1. Tell the student with the defending K to attempt to stay in or near the center to avoid checkmate for as long as possible. Advise the students who are assigned white to coordinate their R and Q in the pattern that was shown on the demonstration board. Driving the defending king to the edge of the board for checkmate may be easy for some students.

After the student with the white pieces successfully executes the checkmate, return to the black (defending) K on e5, the white R on h1, and the white Q on d1 position. Then the other student in the pair, who had been playing the moves of the defending king, takes over the white pieces to practice the checkmate.

If no checkmates have been achieved by either partner, re-teach the mate to that pair of students. If one partner understands but the other does not, have the partner with understanding re-teach the mating pattern to the other.

If the exercise is completed early by some pairs, have them substitute a white K for the white R. Then they can attempt the K and Q versus K checkmate, which is outlined in the section "Computers and Checkmates" in chapter 2 of this book.

Evaluation: Monitor the pairs to see if the players with white are able to checkmate with Q and R versus K. See if they coordinate the rook and the queen in the ladder-style or rolling-pieces checkmate pattern that you demonstrated, that is one file or rank apart with the rook closer to the enemy king. After the pieces are coordinated, the pattern of rook check, queen check, rook check, and so forth should ensue. Optional: To make the connection to thinking backward in math, give the solution to a math problem. Then work with the students to deduce what steps led up to that solution.

♖ Transforming Figures

Objectives: Using chess pawns and pieces to mark the perimeter of an original figure, students rotate, slide, or flip the figure to produce a congruent shape. Then the students find a checkmate in one move in the resulting shape.

Materials: One photocopy of Figure 3.25 for every two students; set and board for every two students; pencils.

Procedure: Pair the students and pass out a board and set to each pair. Call out the following coordinates and piece/pawn names for students to create the parallelogram in Figure 3.26: White Ke5, white Bs on d5 and c7, white Pb7, white Rb6; black Ka7; P's on c5 and d6. Using the fifth

TRANSFORMING FIGURES

Copy the preimage on your chessboard. Transform the preimage as directed. Then find a checkmate for white in one move in the image. Write the checkmate move in notation in the blank space to the right of the appropriate diagram.

Preimage #1

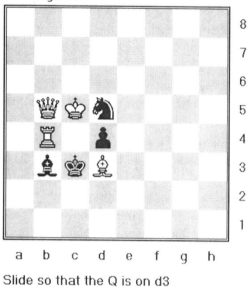

Slide so that the Q is on d3

Preimage #2 Rotate counter-clockwise

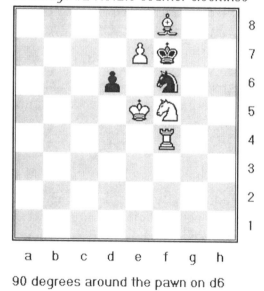

90 degrees around the pawn on d6

Figure 3.25.
Transforming figures worksheet.

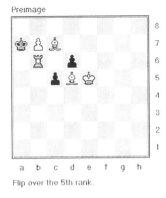

Preimage

Flip over the 5th rank.

Figure 3.26.

Position after flipping over the 5th rank

White to move and mate in 1

Figure 3.27.

rank as a line of reflection, ask students to flip this preimage. The students' boards should now look like Figure 3.27. Give each pair of students five minutes to figure out white's checkmate in one move. Then ask for the answer, 1. Ra4#. Then pass out the "Transforming figures" worksheet (Figure 3.25) to every student.

Evaluation: Check the worksheet using the answer key in Appendix B.

Chapter 4

INTERDISCIPLINARY

Content Connections

In 1982 University of Puget Sound English professor Esther Wagner
(d. 1989) gave me *The Chicken Book* (1975) by Page Smith and Charles
Daniel. At first *The Chicken Book* was meaningful to me because it
was from my favorite undergraduate professor. Twenty years later *The
Chicken Book* helped me see that chess was like the chicken. Smith, a
historian, and Daniel, a biologist, described their university-level chicken
course:

> The class was divided into small groups, each of which pursued a particu-
> lar aspect of that remarkable fowl—the biology and embryology of the
> chicken, the chicken in art, in song, in folklore and literature, in its historic
> and economic and anthropological aspects, the history of the chicken, the
> keeping of ornamental birds, the history of cockfighting, the cooking and
> eating of the chicken and the egg. (Smith & Daniel, 1975, p. 3)

Chess, like the chicken, can be the subject of an interdisciplinary
book or project. Authors David Shenk (2006) and Marilyn Yalom (2004)
connected chess to culture, science, math, history, art, education, and lei-
sure. As a culminating individual or small-group project, students might
research these chess connections. Students pursuing their varied topics
would result in multiple outcomes.

To inspire such research projects, the activities in this chapter link chess to language arts and social studies in addition to math and science. Each student may be attracted by different elements of a particular activity. For example, after hearing *The King's Chessboard* (Birch, 1988/1993), some students might want to learn about how chess developed in India, or to investigate the connection between chess and royalty, or to read other chess fables. But after my son William learned from his older sister how to solve the math problem in "The King's Chessboard" activity, he spent his free time in school the next day calculating three to the thirtieth power. The new math ideas excited him because he'd only been briefly exposed to exponents in his fifth-grade class. "The King's Chessboard," like other chapter 4 activities, teaches its listed objectives. In addition, the activities may motivate students' further educational investigations.

Learning Chess Pieces

Subjects: Math, language arts, social studies. This activity is based on a lesson plan written by Alicia Guzzardo, the University of Texas at Dallas, November, 2006.

Objectives: The student uses attributes to identify, compare, and contrast three-dimensional geometric figures. Also, the student progresses from informal to formal language to describe three-dimensional geometric figures. The student discusses the meanings of words, develops vocabulary through historical references, spells the names of the **chessmen,** and sets up the board in its starting position.

Materials: Set in a cloth bag or opaque box and a board for each pair of students. One set, demonstration board, and a dry-erase board for the teacher. Pencil and paper for each student for taking spelling notes.

Procedure: Say, "Today we are going to learn the names of chess pieces, part of a game that has been around for more than 1,500 years!" Next, explain that students are going to first learn the shapes and names of the six types of chessmen. Then pass out a bagged or boxed set and a board to each student pair, leaving one of the sets for you.

Display the king, queen, and knight, asking students to hold the king, the queen, and the knight in turn. Within each pair's set, students can hold up either a white or a black example of the requested chess figure. Tell students the name of each piece, spell it on the dry-erase board, and ask students to share what they know about that piece. Tell students that the pieces and pawns relate to medieval European history. If not already mentioned by the students, comment that the shapes of the king, queen, and knight correspond to their historical roles. The king and queen have crowns and the knight is shaped like a knight's horse.

Ask students to pick up the pawn while you also pick up a pawn. Have the students comment on its shape attributes and its historical role. Steer the students' answers toward the observation that a pawn has a sphere on top of a cylinder and has a short height. Explain that the pawn is like the peasant in the middle ages, which students may have deduced from the pawn's small stature. Repeat the procedure of you and the students holding up each piece with the rook and the bishop, remembering to ask for students' observations about each piece. Note that the rook has a cylindrical shape. Its top has four notches in it, representing the directions that the rook can move (vertically and horizontally). The rook resembles the tower of a medieval castle. The bishop has a cone shape on top, with a diagonal slash in it. Some people remember how the bishop moves by noticing this diagonal slash. The slash represents the Catholic bishop's miter.

Make sure you have said aloud each piece and pawn name and spelled them on the dry-erase board. At this point in the presentation, have the students copy the names of the chessmen on their papers. Then erase the dry-erase board.

Compare your three-dimensional set with the two-dimensional demonstration board set, so that students recognize the two-dimensional forms of the pieces and pawns. The demonstration board should be arranged with all the pieces and pawns in their starting positions.

Each pair of students already has a box or cloth bag, a set, and a board. Each pair should also have two spelling lists of chessmen. The first student in the pair places one of each type of piece or pawn in the box/bag and holds the pair's spelling papers. The other (second) student draws out a piece or a pawn and spells its name out loud. The first student then checks the spelling by looking at their papers. Then they reverse roles.

Evaluation: Walk around the room during the spelling practice, checking that each piece and pawn is correctly recognized and spelled. For example, students may confuse the king and the queen. Or the students may spell pawn as "pond." As pairs finish spelling the names of the chessmen, tell them to arrange their set in the same manner as the demonstration board. Check to see that the starting position on the demonstration board was accurately copied. Then ask the students to put away the sets and boards.

♟ Map My School on a Board

Subjects: Math, geography.

Objective: Students "make a map on a coordinate system of the various routes they use" (NCTM, 2000, p. 201) to walk from their classroom to other locations in the school.

Materials: Class set of Figure 4.1, pencils, school with straight hallways. Optional teacher resources: Basman (2001, p. 13), King (2000, p. 18), and Polgar (2006, p. 2) also compared chess squares to map-grid squares.

Procedure: Ask the students to imagine that they are now rooks, and can move only vertically and horizontally. As the class proceeds to a special area (art, music, or P.E.) or to lunch, instruct the students to count

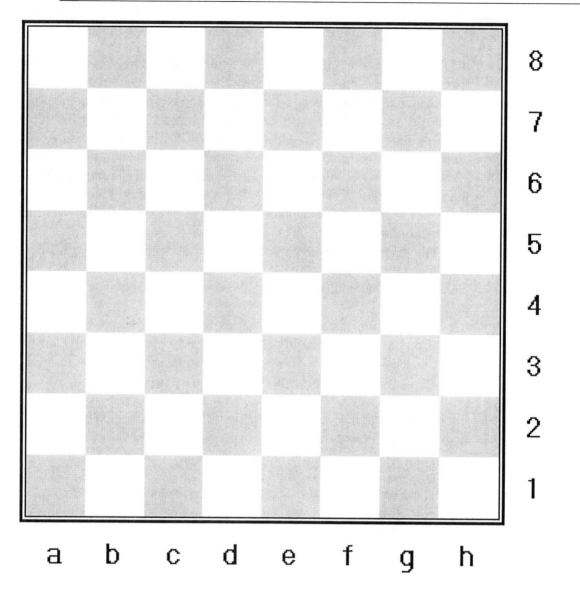

Directions (Write answers to the items listed in **boldface** type):

1) Figure out how many footsteps are represented by each square. For example, if it took 60 footsteps to reach Y from X, then perhaps each square could represent 10 footsteps.

2) Fill in your key here: **One square = _____ footsteps.**

3) On the chessboard, traveling north means to move from the first to the eighth rank; going south is from the eighth to the first rank. Traveling from west to east means starting on the a-file (west) and moving toward the h-file (east). You are a rook and move only along ranks and files. **Mark your classroom with an X. Mark the location of the destination room with a Y.**

4) **Draw your route using a line through the middle of the squares traveled from X to Y.**

Figure 4.1.
Map your school on the board.

how many footsteps in each direction it took to get from the door of their classroom to the destination. For simplicity, tell the students when they are heading east, west, north, or south. For example, to get from my son William's fifth-grade classroom to the cafeteria it took about 50 steps east and 10 steps north.

Collect data from students and work with them to average it. To continue the same example, William (and others) counted 60 steps east while Hailey (and others) counted 40 steps east. Help the class average the steps taken, calling on students to work each part of the averaging problem on the dry-erase board. The average should be rounded to the nearest even, whole number for each direction walked. Then each student is given a copy of Figure 4.1. Using the data agreed upon by the class, the individual student decides where the classroom and the destination are located on the board, how many steps each square counts for, and traces the rook route taken by him and his classmates from X to Y.

Evaluation: Do students understand north, south, east, west, vertical, and horizontal? During the discussion on averaging the footsteps, did students seem to understand the procedure for averaging? Did they understand why the average was rounded to the nearest even, whole number? Did the key created by each student make sense? Did the route drawn on the board correspond to the actual route taken from X to Y in school?

♟ The Knights Can't Wait!

Subjects: Literature, math.

Objectives: Students reenact on the board the plot of the first-grade book *Coco Can't Wait!*, by developing a pattern of knights' moves that (almost) fits the story requirements. Students pay attention to "the geometry of the board itself along with the particular way in which knights are allowed to move," components of graph theory (Watkins, 2004, p. 3). Students discuss solutions to the real-life problem of how to meet someone.

Materials: Coco Can't Wait! (Gomi, 1993), demonstration board, enough boards and sets so that every group of two to four students can have a set with two different-colored knights. If you can't find a copy of *Coco Can't Wait!*, I've provided a story summary in the Procedure section of this activity. You can teach the activity using this summary. Optional (for the extension): notebook paper or copies of Figure 1.6 (score sheets) and pencils for each group. MacEnulty (2006, p. 121) describes a "horse race," a competitive activity where knights attempt to reach particular squares first. My activity utilizes the same chess concept but is cooperative.

Procedure: Ask students if they've ever had the experience of wishing to see someone, going to where they think that person is, and finding out that the person has just left. Allow students to share a couple of stories. Read the first part of *Coco Can't Wait!* Here is the summary of the first part of the story: Coco is a little girl who wants to see her Grandma. She begins to travel to Grandma's home. At the same time, Grandma wants to see Coco. So Grandma leaves her home to see Coco at Coco's home. When Grandma arrives at Coco's home, she is told that Coco has left for Grandma's home. And when Coco arrives at Grandma's house, Grandpa tells her that Grandma is not present. End this part of the read-aloud with, "Oh no! Grandma is not here!" (Gomi, 1993, p. 15).

Tell the students that the white knight on b1 and the black knight on b8 are like Coco and her Grandma. The white knight on b1, Coco, moves first. Then the black knight on b8, Grandma, moves. Both head to each other's home squares. For teaching this lesson to most students, have Coco knight arrive at Grandma's home a half-move before Grandma arrives at Coco's home without commenting on the mismatch with the story.

For gifted students, point out that in the story Grandma appears to arrive at Coco's home before Coco arrives at Grandma's home. Ask if chess can represent Grandma's earlier arrival (see Appendix B).

On the demonstration board, run through a sample route with the class, allowing them to suggest moves for both the Coco knight and the Grandma knight. Correct and instruct as necessary regarding the legal moves of the knight, telling students that knights move in a capital L-shape. Knights also start and end each move on a different-colored square. For this story, Coco capturing Grandma (or Grandma capturing Coco) is not allowed. The moves alternate between Coco and Grandma. After the class understands how a knight moves, as shown by class members' suggesting correct moves for Coco and Grandma, review the requirements for "The Knights Can't Wait":

1. Start the white knight on b1 and the black knight on b8.
2. The white knight (Coco) moves first.
3. Students in each group should help each other so that the white knight (from b1) finishes on b8 a half-move before the black knight (from b8) ends on b1.
4. The route the knights take can be as short or as elaborate as the students want, as long as the condition in step three is met.
5. No captures are allowed.
6. As an extension, or for older or more experienced chess or math students, have one member of the group track the moves of Coco knight and Grandma knight, using notation on a score sheet (Figure 1.6) or notebook paper.

Pass out one board and two opposite-colored knights to each small group of students. If you are having students try step six above, pass out pencils and paper or score sheets (Figure 1.6). If some groups are faster than others, have the faster groups reverse the direction of the knights (return each knight to its home square).

Collect the knights and boards and read the end of the story. Here is a summary of the end of the story: After Coco and her Grandma fail to find each other, they return to their own homes. They learn that they've just missed each other, and race off toward each other's homes again. Luckily, this time they meet each other in the middle. Ask students how to solve the problem of meeting someone. They might offer some of the following suggestions: have a fixed meeting place and time, call each other, use walkie-talkies, stay put so that the person can find you, or use a tracking device or beeper.

Evaluation: Walk around while students are in groups to see if they are moving the knights legally and accomplishing the task. Ask students what feelings the words and artwork of *Coco Can't Wait!* evoked. Assess the practicality and safety of the suggestions students offered for meeting someone.

If the extension in step six was attempted, ask students to show their routes and discuss route efficiency. And, with gifted students, discuss what pieces or pawns Coco and Grandma need to be to meet the story requirements exactly (see Appendix B).

♟ The King's Chessboard

Subjects: Math, language arts.

Objectives: Students listen to your reading of *The King's Chessboard* and comprehend the selection using a variety of strategies. The students reason mathematically about the doubling question posed by *The King's Chessboard.*

Materials: The King's Chessboard (Birch, 1988/1993), calculators, pencils, paper, one copy of Figure 3.3 (the blank chess diagram) for each small group. If you can't find a copy of *The King's Chessboard,* I've provided story summaries in the Procedure section of this activity. You will be able to teach the activity using the story summaries.

Procedure: Read the book aloud until the end of page nine, or tell the first part of the story. Here is a summary of the first part: A wise man performed valuable services for the king of India. The king asked the wise man what reward he required. The wise man said none, but the king insisted. So the wise man requested that one grain of rice be placed on the first chess square, two on the second square, four on the third square, and then a continuation of doubling the rice grains on each subsequent square until the 64th square.

End this part of your reading with, "There was much amusement at this simple old man and his odd request" (Birch, 1988/1993, p. 9). Then assign students to groups of three to five to answer the question, "How many grains of rice will be placed on the 64th square?" Pass out calculators, pencils, copies of Figure 3.3, and paper. Before the members of each small group start work, ask them to write "1" on whichever square they think the king put the first grain of rice. Then have them write "2" on the adjacent square, to indicate the two grains on the second day. Ask them to use the Figure 3.3 diagram squares to record the grains of rice, and the paper and calculator to make other calculations as needed.

Circulate among the groups to listen to their mathematical communication and to observe their calculations. Provide hints as you see fit. Some groups may come to the following correct solution: Starting on the second day, there are two grains; On the third day, on the third square, four grains of rice will be placed (two to the second power); On the fourth day/square, eight grains (two to the third power); On the fifth day/square, 16 grains (two to the fourth power); Therefore, on the 64th day/square, there will be two to the 63rd power grains placed on the 64th square, or 9,223,372,036,854,775,808.

After you feel the groups have spent enough time attempting to solve the problem, ask groups to share their solutions. Then share the solution above, if it hasn't already been mentioned. Then read the rest of the story to the class. The conclusion of the story takes place after the 32nd square has been filled, and the king has realized that he doesn't have enough rice for the rest of the squares. He asks the wise man if he is satisfied. The wise man says that he always was; it was the king who wanted to give a reward.

Evaluation: Did the students work productively in the groups? Did students see the doubling pattern square to square? Did the students understand the exponent-based solution? Plan a similar problem for another day to see if students transfer their newfound understanding.

♞ How to Castle

Subjects: Science, language arts.

Objectives: Students write a "how-to" essay, describing the reasons, procedures, and conditions for castling. Students practice writing in the same "how-to" style used in the methodology section of lab reports and for science fair projects.

Materials: Demonstration board. Set and board for every two students. For each student, notebook paper and pencils (for writing essays). Dry-erase board. Optional teacher resource: Review the chapter 5 section on castling before teaching this activity.

Procedure: Review prior instruction on writing "how-to" essays. For example, when my daughter Clarissa was in the fourth grade, students wrote an essay on how to make a peanut-butter sandwich. Then the teacher followed the instructions in one student's essay with actual ingredients (bread, peanut butter, jam) to see if a sandwich resulted. If such a writing assignment has already been attempted, review how that assignment went.

If science fair is coming up, you might also show a poster board from a past science fair winner. Highlight the methodology section of the winning science fair poster. Show how each step is listed in the order in which it was performed. Note the importance of "how-to" writing in cooking (making the peanut-butter sandwich) and in science (steps of an experiment). "How-to" essays also state or imply why the activity described is important. For example, following the sandwich steps means that you'll have an edible sandwich. Recording experimental steps correctly allows other researchers to replicate your experiment.

State that today students will learn why castling is important and how to castle. Tell students that they will be writing an essay based on five statements written on the dry-erase board. Write the following (numbers 1–5, plus the text in italics) on the board. Call on students for answers. For example, when writing number one on the board, ask students why they think it is good to castle. Then build on their answers with the information in this activity.

1. *Why it is good to castle.* Either **kingside** or **queenside** castling activates the castled rook, bringing it out of the corner and toward the center where files are more likely to be open (free of pawns). Rooks move more easily and powerfully when files are open. At the same time, castling moves kings closer to the corners. After castling, kings are on the g- or c-files. In those locations, they are sheltered by their own f-, g-, and h-pawns (when castled on the kingside) and c-, b-, and a-pawns (when castled on the queenside). It is best not to have moved any of those sheltering pawns. Exceptions are pawn moves to block a checkmate attempt or to **fianchetto** bishops along the long diagonals (a1-h8 and h1-a8).

2. *How to castle kingside.* Use the demonstration board to show how to castle, using Figures 5.8 and 5.9 from chapter 5.

3. *How to castle queenside.* Use the demonstration board to show how to castle, using Figures 5.8 and 5.9 from chapter 5.

4. *Conditions that permit castling.* No pieces in between the king and the rook that is castling with that king. Castling is the first move for that king and the castling rook.

5. *Conditions that prohibit castling.* Set up Figures 4.3, 4.4, and 4.5 on the demonstration board, to show positions where castling is prohibited. WK is the white king, and BK is the black king; 0–0 is kingside castling, and 0–0–0 is queenside castling.

As advice for best chess play, instruct students that they should castle within the first 10 moves. Castling kingside requires moving the f-file bishop and g-file knight off the back rank. Queenside castling requires moving the c-file bishop, b-file knight, and the queen off the back rank. Therefore, castling kingside is faster and more common. Tell students to raise their hands when they

b-pawn moved for black B development

White can 0-0. The Bg2 helps protect K.

Figure 4.2.
Fianchettoed bishops.

Black K is in check and cannot castle.

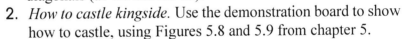

WK can't castle while f1 is being attacked

Figure 4.3.
No castling when in check, or over a check.

BK has moved; black can't castle now.

WK can't 0-0, but can 0-0-0.

Figure 4.4.
No castling into check; no castling if king has moved.

Black R is not on h8, so 0-0 impossible.

BK can 0-0-0, since Ra8 hasn't moved.

Figure 4.5.
No castling on the side where the rook has already moved.

are about to castle so that you can see if they are castling correctly. Pair up students and pass out boards and sets to allow chess playing and castling practice.

Evaluation: For homework or at the end of class, students individually write a "how to castle" essay. Remind students that their essay should include the five topics written on the dry-erase board. Tell students that the audience for their essays knows how kings and rooks move but has not heard of castling.

After you have evaluated the essays, read one or two of them to the class. As you read an essay aloud, follow its castling instructions on the demonstration board. Ask students if the essay covered each aspect of castling. A sample essay is in Appendix B.

♟ Kasparov versus the World

Subjects: Social studies (geography and government), communication, math.

Objectives: Over the course of one or two months, students from one classroom will play a chess game with students from another classroom. Students will vote on each move after speeches by in-class experts. Students will use notation to communicate that chosen move to the opposing classroom. If the opposing class room is from another school, students will learn the geographic location of that school.

Materials: Account of the Kasparov versus the World game, such as http://www.microsoft.com/presspass/press/1999/oct99/kasparovwinspr. mspx, demonstration board, technology to communicate notated move to opposing classroom (Internet, distance learning, mail, or phone).

Procedure: Share with students the story of then–World Chess Champion Garry Kasparov's match with the rest of the world in the fall of 1999. Kasparov and rest of the world each had 24 hours to decide on a move. Kasparov played whichever move he thought was best. When it was the world's turn, four top teenage players advised the world about best-move choices. The 58,000 people who voted for the world's moves took the young masters' advice into account. Nevertheless, the world's move was decided by a democratic vote. In other words, whichever move got the most votes in 24 hours was the move that was actually played against Kasparov. One analogy is that the three judges on the *American Idol* TV show can recommend which singer to vote for, but a vote of the public decides which singer is selected. Ask students whether they think the public, voting democratically, won or lost against Kasparov. Answer: The rest of the world lost, but the game was very close and lasted for 62 moves (four months of play).

Tell students that they will be playing another classroom at chess. Find the location of that classroom on a map. Or, if the classroom is within your school, point out that classroom to your students. Select three classroom experts (students) for the first move of the chess game. Those experts should be volunteers who have knowledge of chess. New experts may be chosen for each subsequent move.

When it is your class's turn to move, let each expert have a two-minute turn at the demonstration board and dry-erase board. The expert should show his or her recommended move on the demonstration board. The expert should explain why that move is a good choice for the class. Class members can ask questions of the expert after his or her presentation. Finally, the expert should write his or her recommended move on the dry-erase board. After all three experts have had their turns to speak, the class (including the experts) votes for its favorite move by a show of hands. The selected move is transmitted, via algebraic notation, to the opposing classroom. That classroom has 24 hours to respond with a move, and then the process repeats. If 24 hours is too fast a turnaround time, then a longer time control—such as one week per move—could be selected.

Evaluation: Look for the experts' communication of chess ideas. For example, when relevant, the expert should refer to your previous chess instruction. Notice whether the class asks thoughtful questions of the experts.

When the game is done, or both teachers feel that enough moves have been played for a useful experience, the two classrooms could conduct a **post mortem** in person, by phone, or by distance learning. As the moves are replayed on demonstration board(s), students will recall what they were thinking on each move. Then give students in each class a chance to communicate, for example to ask their counterparts, "Why did you move the knight on move 13?" or to comment, "Great piece capture on move 10!"

♖ Know More, Move More!

Subject: Teacher's choice academic content.

Objectives: Students review objective questions about an academic content area to prepare for a test on that content. Students practice chess.

Materials: Fifty index cards, with a review question on one side of the card and the answer on the opposite side. To create the review cards, photocopy your usual review sheet or old tests. Cut out the first multiple choice or true/false question and glue it to the front of the index card. Write the answer on the back of the same card. Follow the same procedure for questions 2–50. Optional: Laminate the cards to make them last longer.

Every pair of students needs a set and board and four or five index cards. Class set of score sheets (Figure 1.6 from chapter 1, or other score sheet), notebook paper, and pencil for each student.

Procedure: Tell students that on every move which is a multiple of five (5, 10, 15, 20, 25 . . .), white will make a move and then draw a card to try to earn an extra move. Because of these extra moves, regular chess notation is not required. Simply have students make checkmarks every time white or black makes a regular move, but omit checkmarks for the extra moves earned by answering questions correctly.

On a move that is a multiple of five, white reads the question on the card aloud, without looking at the answer on the back. White works out the problem in his head or on notebook paper and then says the answer out loud. Black checks the answer by looking at the back of the card. If the answer is correct, white makes an extra move. That extra move should not be notated on the score sheet.

Then black makes one reply move and then draws a new card from the pile. Black reads the question on the card aloud, without looking at the answer on the back. Black works out the problem in her head or on notebook paper, then says the answer out loud. White checks the answer by looking at the back of the card. If the answer is correct, black makes an extra move, also not written on the score sheet. Then the chess game proceeds, white move followed by black move, until the next multiple of five is reached on the score sheet. At that point, the scenario of an extra move for a correctly- answered question repeats.

As students use up their original pile of four or five index cards, have them trade their pile with a neighboring pair. In this way, the index cards circulate around the room.

Evaluation: Walk around the room as students play. Observe who plays extra moves: Those students are succeeding on the review questions for the content test. Plan to provide academic help for students who never play extra moves. The extra chess moves should provide an incentive for students to try harder on the review questions, since extra moves make it easier to win a chess game. Thus "Know More, Move More!" might motivate more students than would the same review questions handed out in a worksheet format.

♕ Move Order Mystery

Subjects: Language arts, science.

Objective: Students hypothesize the most logical move order for the first five moves from a familiar chess opening.

Materials: Demonstration board. Set and board for every two students. Figure 4.6, pre-cut moves within move sets along dotted lines, preparing one set of five white and black moves from each opening line for each pair of students. Dry-erase board. Reference: Eade, 2005, pp. 202–206.

Procedure: Teach two opening lines of the Petroff's Defense (Russian Defense). As you teach each of the two opening lines, write the moves on your dry-erase board. First, show the opening **trap** that black might fall into. **Variations** are in regular font. The game's actual moves are in **bold-face.** Opening Line One: **1. e4 e5 2. Nf3 Nf6 3. Nxe5 Nxe4? 4. Qe2** White attacks black's knight on e4. It can be defended with 4….d5. Then white would play 5. d3. If the black knight moves away from the pawn's attack,

These two Opening Lines are from the Petroff's (Russian) Defense. Line One, when put in the correct order, shows a common trap that black may fall into in this opening. Line Two is a good move order for black.

Opening Line One (cut along each dotted line for half of the pairs in the classroom):

e4	e5
Nf3	Nf6
Nxe5	Nxe4
Qe2	Nf6
Nc6+	resigns

Opening Line Two (cut along each dotted line for half the pairs in the classroom):

e4	e5
Nf3	Nf6
Nxe5	d6
Nf3	Nxe4
Qe2	Qe7

Figure 4.6.
Chess moves from the Russian Defense.

From *Science, Math, Checkmate: 32 Chess Activities for Inquiry and Problem Solving* by Alexey W. Root. Westport, CT: Teacher Ideas Press. Copyright © 2008.

the resulting moves would be similar to the game. Best instead is 4....Qe7 5. Qxe4 d6 6. d4, and White will be a pawn ahead. **4....Nf6 5. Nc6+ (discovered check).** The knight, by moving to c6, unveiled the queen's check. **5....resigns.** Black loses his queen for a knight, since white's next move will be NxQ (on either d8 or, if the Q moves to e7, on e7).

Second, show correct play for black. Again, the game's notation is in **boldface,** and variations are in regular font. Opening Line Two: **1. e4 e5 2. Nf3 Nf6 3. Nxe5 d6** This move forces white's knight to retreat. In this level position, one would not surrender a knight (worth 3 points) for a pawn (worth 1 point). **4. Nf3 Nxe4 5. Qe2** This move attacks black's knight. Black needs to defend the knight, because it is **pinned** to the black king. **5....Qe7** Now if white's knight moves there is no discovered check on the black king.

Other move orders are possible but not logical. For example, games sometimes start with **1. Nf3 Nf6.** But then **2. e4** would not make sense, because black would play **2....Nxe4** winning a pawn. Therefore, the opening sequence logically has to be **1. e4 e5 2. Nf3 Nf6.**

Have each pair of students play one practice game that starts with Opening Line Two of the Petroff's Defense. Students look at the dry-erase board to replicate the first five moves. Then they continue the game on their own, with white to move, on move six.

Evaluation: The next day, or later in the week, pair up students and hand each pair a set, board, and a collection of five white and black moves (either Opening Line One or Opening Line Two) from Figure 4.6. Ask the pairs to put the moves in the most logical, legal order. They may experiment with different orders, moving their pieces around accordingly. Though this move order mystery activity reviews your Petroff's instruction, students may have forgotten the exact move order. When the pair agrees on a move order, they should play out their moves for you to check their answer. If the pair is correct, let them observe or assist other pairs.

The next activity also involves students in the study of chess openings. For my Openings around the World week at chess camps, I demonstrated the moves of a different opening variation each day. When showing the moves of each opening, I emphasized the ABCD opening principles (my acronym):

1. **A**ttack the center;
2. **B**ishops and knights, in either order, should be developed before rooks and queens;
3. **C**astle within the first 10 moves for king safety and to activate the rooks; and
4. **D**elay queen development, so that the queen doesn't become a target. To develop as chess players, students should learn and practice the ABCD principles of correct opening play.

♛ Openings around the World

Subjects: Social studies, history of science.

Objectives: Students memorize the first 8 to 12 moves of a chess opening named after a country or region. Students read about a scientist, science movement, or scientific achievement from that country or region. Optional: Provide social studies information about the country or region.

Materials: Demonstration board. Dry-erase board. Set and board for every two students. Paper or score sheets (Figure 1.6) and pencils for each student. Library books, articles, or Web sites about a scientist, science movement, or scientific achievement from the country or region of the chess opening of the day. Optional: Include library books, articles, or Web sites that show the history and culture of the region.

When I taught Openings around the World at chess camps, I used the following chess references:

- Day One: the Italian Game, Giuoco Piano variation (Seirawan, 1998, pp. 47–48);
- Day Two: the Italian Game, Evans Gambit variation (Seirawan, 1998, pp. 46–47);
- Day Three: the Sicilian Defense, Dragon variation (Wolff, 2005, pp. 167–171); and
- Day Four: the Russian Defense, also known as Petroff's Defense, (Seirawan, 1998, p. 40).

Appendix B gives a sample opening line from the Sicilian Defense, Dragon variation.

Procedure: Tell students that today they will memorize a chess opening that is named after a country or region, and then read about a scientist, science movement, or scientific achievement from that country. Explain that several chess openings are named after countries and regions. For example, the French Defense, the Italian Game, the Latvian Gambit, the Sicilian Defense, the Russian Defense, the English Opening, the Scandinavian Defense, the Scotch Opening, the Danish Gambit, the Polish Opening, and the Spanish Game. Optional: Provide social studies information about the country or region of the opening of the day.

Show the moves of the opening on the demonstration board, and simultaneously write the moves in algebraic notation on the dry-erase board. Students copy the moves on notebook paper, or on Figure 1.6 or other score sheet. As you show the moves, ask students how they fit with the ABCD principles of correct opening play. If the students have questions about particular moves, you may quote answers from authors such as Seirawan (1998) and Wolff (2005). The cited chess authors explain the first 8–12 moves for different openings. Stop writing moves on the same move that the author stops his explanation.

Students are paired, given a set and board, and told to memorize the given number of moves in that particular opening. Erase the dry-erase board. Using their notes and chess equipment, the pairs replay the algebraic moves that they've copied. After five minutes or so, pairs who think that they have memorized the moves should raise their hands. You then hold their papers, using them as an answer key as the students replay the opening. The students must show the opening twice, switching colors for the second time. In this way, each student shows that he or she has memorized the opening from both the white side and the black side. If the either member of the pair fails, the pair must review for five minutes before asking you to retest them. If the pair succeeds in recreating the opening's moves, certify both members of the pair. Those students who are certified may then use their memorized knowledge and their written notes to test other students. Once there are several more certified students than pairs remaining to be tested, direct the certified students to pack up their chess equipment and begin their science reading. When the remaining pairs have memorized the opening, you will certify them.

As students finish certification, direct their attention to the history of science portion of the activity. Students should silently read through the materials that you have provided. For example, you might have biographical information about Galileo and information about the history of Italy available on the day your students learn the Italian game.

Evaluation: The evaluation of students' memorization of the chess opening takes place within this activity. Students must memorize each opening such that they can reproduce it correctly, from both the white side and the black side, without hints or taking back moves. In other words, students silently demonstrate the memorized opening following "touch-move" protocol. For the science or social studies portion of the lesson, students should read quietly.

Chapter 5

CHESS BASICS

Rules of Chess

Let's Play Chess

Chess is a game for two players, one with the white pieces and one with the black pieces. In this chapter, the term "pieces" refers to both the pieces and pawns. In the rest of *Science, Math, Checkmate,* and in many other chess texts, pieces refer to the kings, queens, rooks, bishops, and knights only. Pawns are called pawns. At the beginning of the game, the pieces are set up as shown in Figure 5.1. These hints will help you remember the proper board setup:

1. Opposing kings and queens go directly opposite each other.
2. The square in the lower right hand corner is a light (white) one. Remember the expression "light on right."
3. The white queen goes on a light square, and the black queen on a dark square.

The Pieces and How They Move

White always moves first, and then the players take turns moving. Only one piece may be moved at each turn (except for castling, as explained later in the chapter under the heading "Special Moves").

Starting position of a chess game.

Queen on her own color.

Figure 5.1.

The knight is the only piece that can jump over other pieces. All other pieces move only along unblocked lines. You may not move a piece to a square already occupied by one of your own pieces. But you may capture an opponent's piece that stands on a square where one of your pieces can move. Simply remove the opponent's piece from the board and put your own piece in its place (except for the en passant pawn capture, as explained in "Special Moves"). Although touching pieces and pawns may be helpful when practicing chess drills or solving chess problems, the touch move rule should apply in every chess game or chess drill where wins, losses, and draws are recorded.

The values of the pieces provide a guideline for whether a particular capture is a correct decision. Generally speaking, the side with the stronger army will win. The strength of your army is determined by its point value. For example, trading a knight (worth three points) for a queen (worth nine points) is usually a good idea, because the **trade** leaves you the equivalent of six points ahead. The value of a pawn is one point, so a knight is worth three pawns or three points.

■ *The King*

The king is the most important piece, and has the symbol K. The graphic ♔ represents the white king, and ♚ is the black king. As discussed in the section "About Check, Checkmate, and Stalemate," when the king is checkmated his whole army loses. Therefore, in one sense, the king's point value is infinite. However, his actual value as an attacking force is generally about three points according to Wolff (2005, p. 76) and close to four points in the endgame according to USCF and Kurzdorfer (2003, p. 96). The king can move one square in any direction—for example, to any of the squares with Xs in Figure 5.2. The king may never move into check—that is, onto a square attacked by an opponent's piece. If conditions are correct, the king may castle once per game (explained in "Special Moves").

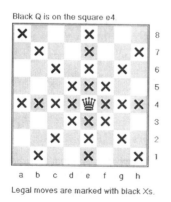

Black K on e8 can move to black Xs.

White K on c3 can move to white Xs.

Figure 5.2.
Moves of the king (K).

Black Q is on the square e4

Legal moves are marked with black Xs.

Figure 5.3.
Moves of the queen (Q).

■ *The Queen*

The queen is the most powerful piece, and has the symbol Q. The graphic ♕ represents the white queen, and ♛ is the black queen. The queen is worth nine points. If her path is not blocked, the queen can move any number of squares horizontally, vertically, or diagonally. She can reach any of the squares with black Xs in Figure 5.3.

■ *The Rook*

The rook is the next most powerful piece, and has the symbol R. The graphic ♖ represents the white rooks, and ♜ symbolizes

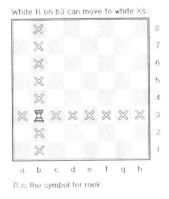

Figure 5.4.
Moves of the rook (R).

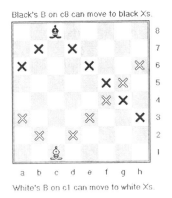

Figure 5.5.
Moves of the bishop (B).

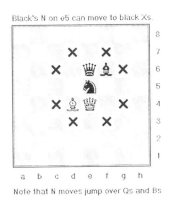

Figure 5.6.
Moves of the knight (N).

the black rooks. The rook is worth five points. The rook can move any number of squares vertically or horizontally if its path is not blocked. The rook can reach any of the squares with white Xs in Figure 5.4.

■ *The Bishop*

The bishop has the symbol B, and has the graphic ♗ for white's bishops and ♝ for black's bishops. The bishop is generally considered to be worth three points, though some chess writers place the bishop's value slightly higher. For example, Wolff (2005, p. 75) wrote, "3 points (plus a teensy bit more)." The bishop can move any number of squares diagonally if its path is not blocked. At the beginning of the game, each side has one light-squared bishop and one dark-squared bishop. In Figure 5.5, the white bishop on c1 is white's dark- or black-squared bishop. It must stay on the black squares, marked by white Xs. In Figure 5.5, black's bishop on c8 is a light or white-squared bishop. It can move to the white squares marked by black Xs.

■ *The Knight*

The knight has the symbol N, and has the graphic ♘ for white's knights and ♞ for black's knights. The knight is worth three points. The knight hops over any pieces in between its old and new squares. Think of the knight's move as the capital letter "L." It moves two squares horizontally or vertically and then makes a right-angle turn for one more square. The knight always lands on a square opposite in color from its prior square. Figure 5.6 shows the N's moves with black Xs.

■ *The Pawn*

The pawn has the symbol P, but generally pawn moves are notated by stating the square the pawn moves to without use of the P. The graphic symbol for the white pawns is ♙, and the symbol for the black pawns is ♟. A pawn is worth one point (one pawn). The pawn moves straight ahead (never backward), but it captures diagonally. It moves one square at a time, but on its first move it has the option of moving forward one or two squares.

In Figure 5.7, the circles indicate possible destinations for the pawns. The white pawn is on its original square, so it may move ahead either one or two squares. The black pawn has previously moved, so it may move ahead only one square at a time. The squares on which these pawns may make captures are indicated by Xs. However, captures would only be possible if enemy pieces were on the X-ed squares.

Black P can move to g4.

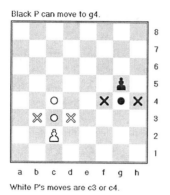

White P's moves are c3 or c4.

Figure 5.7.
Moves of the pawn (P).

If a pawn advances to the opposite end of the board, it is immediately promoted to another piece. It may not remain a pawn or become a king. One can promote a pawn to a queen (or R, or N, or B) even if one still has the original piece(s) on the board. In Figure 5.7, the promotion square for the white pawn is c8 and the promotion square for the black pawn is g1.

Special Moves

There are two special moves in the game of chess. The first, castling, occurs in almost every chess game contested between experienced chess players. The second, en passant, is possible in less than 1 game out of 10 (USCF & Kurzdorfer, 2003, p. 62).

■ *Castling*

Each player may castle only once during a game, when certain conditions are met. Castling is a special move that lets a player move two pieces at once: the king and one rook. Castling allows you to place your king in a safe location and also allows the castled rook to become more active. When the move is legal, each player has the choice of castling kingside or queenside or not at all, no matter what the other player chooses to do.

The procedure for castling is to move your king two squares to his left or right, toward one of his rooks. At the same time, the rook involved goes to the square beside the king and toward the center of the board. Kingside castling is sometimes called "castling short" and queenside castling is "castling long" (Khmelnitsky, Khodarkovsky, & Zadorozny, 2006, Book 1, p. 89; King, 2000, p. 26). Figures 5.8 and 5.9 show castling.

In order to castle, neither the king nor the rook involved may have moved before. Also, the king may not castle out of check, into check, or through check. Furthermore, there may not be pieces of either color between the king and the rook involved in castling. See the "How to Castle" activity from chapter 4 for chess diagrams of prohibited castling positions.

Black before kingside castling.

White before queenside castling.

Figure 5.8.
Before castling.

■ *En Passant (e.p.)*

This French phrase, meaning "in passing," is used to describe a special pawn capture. When one player moves a pawn two squares forward so that it is on an adjacent rank and file to an opponent's pawn, that opponent's pawn can capture the double-jumping pawn as if it had only moved one square. However, if the opponent's pawn does not exercise the en passant capture immediately, the option disappears for that particular e.p. capture. But new opportunities may arise for each pawn in similar circumstances.

Black after kingside castling.

White after queenside castling.

Figure 5.9.
After castling.

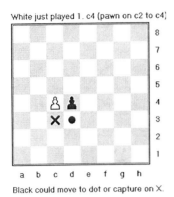

White just played 1. c4 (pawn on c2 to c4)

Black could move to dot or capture on X.

Figure 5.10.
The en passant (e.p.) rule.

The rule originated when pawns gained the double-jump power on their first move, which occurred shortly after the 1450s (King, 2000, pp. 8, 27). Reflecting a desire to keep some consistency despite the rule change, the en passant rule arose so that one could capture the double-jump pawn as if it had only moved one square. Figure 5.10 shows black's choices. If black takes en passant (1....dxc3 e.p.), his black pawn ends up on c3 and white's pawn on c4 is removed from the board. For more examples, see "To e.p. or not to e.p." in chapter 2.

About Check, Checkmate, and Stalemate

The ultimate goal of chess is to checkmate your opponent's king. The king is not actually captured and removed from the board like other pieces. But if the king is attacked (checked), it must get out of check immediately. If there is no way to get out of check, then the position is a checkmate. The side that is checkmated loses.

You may not move into check. For example, moving into a direct line with your opponent's rook if there are no other pieces between the rook and your king is an illegal move. Otherwise, the rook could "capture" your king, which is not allowed.

If you are put into check by your opponent's move, there are three ways of getting out of check:

1. Capture the attacking piece;
2. Place one of your own pieces between the attacker and your king. Blockading doesn't work if the attacker is a knight or a pawn;
3. Move your king away from the attack.

If a checked player has none of these three escapes, then he is checkmated and loses the game. In a chess tournament, a checkmate is scored as a win (one point) for the player delivering the checkmate.

In contrast, if a player is not in check but has no legal move, the position is called a stalemate. A stalemate is scored as a draw or tie (half a point) for each player.

These preceding rules of chess were adapted from *Let's Play Chess* (USCF, 2004) and are used with permission of the United States Chess Federation http://www.uschess.org. The next two sections of chapter 5— "Win, Lose, or Draw" and "Reading and Writing Chess"—illustrate what happens when chess games are underway.

Win, Lose, or Draw

As noted in the rules of chess, games end when checkmate or stalemate occurs. A check, however, is temporary. When the king escapes from check, the game continues. Figure 5.11 has exercises to identify

For each diagram, tell whether the position is a check, a mate (checkmate), or a stalemate. Write your answer in the space below the diagram.

Black to move. Check, mate, or stalemate

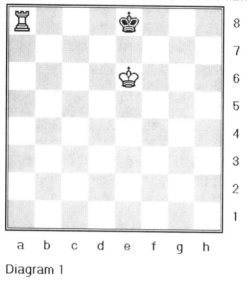

Diagram 1

Black to move. Check, mate, or stalemate

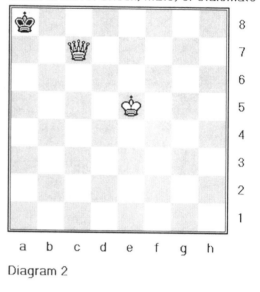

Diagram 2

White to move. Check, mate, or stalemate

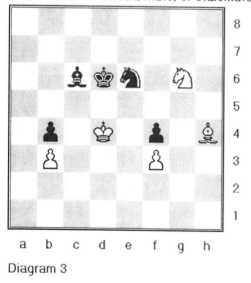

Diagram 3

White to move. Check, mate, or stalemate

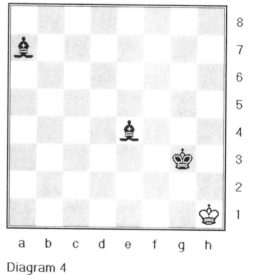

Diagram 4

Figure 5.11.
Check, checkmate, or stalemate?

check, checkmate, and stalemate. The answer key for Figure 5.11 is in Appendix B. Stalemate is just one of several ways that chess games can be drawn; see *draws* in the Glossary.

In addition to losing by being checkmated, you can also lose a game by resigning (giving up). Beginners should usually continue playing until checkmate rather than resigning. Although wins keep your spirits up and allow you to practice checkmating, losses educate by showing you where your chess moves went wrong.

Reading and Writing Chess

Playing chess games is one way to improve at chess; learning chess notation is another improvement method. Reading notation enables you to study games published in chess columns in newspapers, in chess magazines, and in chess books. Notating your own chess games allows you to review those games later with a friend, parent, teacher, or chess coach. Two Web sites that teach algebraic chess notation, the most common notating system today, are http://chess.about.com/od/ beginners/ss/ble21brd.htm and http://www.uschess.org/about/forms/ KEEPINGSCORE.pdf.

Here is an example of algebraic notation from a common chess opening, the Ruy Lopez, Exchange variation:

1. e4 e5 2. Nf3 Nc6 3. Bb5 a6 4. Bxc6 dxc6 5. 0–0 Bg4

Now I will explain how each move was notated. **1. e4** Figure 5.12 shows the move 1. e4 on the board. The white pawn that sits in front of the white king moved two squares forward. The square is named e4, derived from the file name (e) and the rank name (4). When a pawn (P) moves there, we could write Pe4, but it is traditional not to list the P when notating pawn moves. **1....e5** The ellipses (...) before the move lets us know that the pawn move e5 was a move for black. Figure 5.13 shows the position after black moved the pawn in front of his king two squares forward. **2. Nf3** From the "f3" we know that some piece has moved to f3, but which one? N stands for knight, so it is the knight that white moved from g1 to f3. The position after white's second move is shown in Figure 5.14. **2....Nc6** Black replied with a knight's move from b8 to c6. The resulting position is shown in Figure 5.15. **3. Bb5** B stands for bishop, which white moved from f1 to b5. The resulting position is shown in Figure 5.16. Now follow the next couple of moves in your head or on a board. **3....a6 4. Bxc6** The "x" means capture. **4....dxc6** Notice that either the b-pawn or the d-pawn could have recaptured the white B on c6. 4....dxc6 tells us that the d-pawn recaptured. **5. 0–0** This notation means kingside castling. You can

Figure 5.12.

Figure 5.13.

2. Nf3 Knight moves to the square f3

White's second move

Figure 5.14.

2....Nc6 Knight moves to the square c6

Black's second move

Figure 5.15.

3. Bb5 Bishop moves to the square b5.

White's third move

Figure 5.16.

Ruy Lopez, Exchange Variation

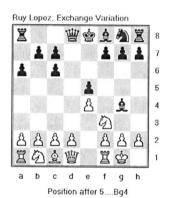

Position after 5....Bg4

Figure 5.17.

use zeroes or capital letter O's for castling. Queenside castling is written 0-0-0. Two other special symbols are +, written at the end of a move to show that the move gave a check; # or + + designates giving checkmate. **5....Bg4** Black's fifth move is bishop to the square g4. The position after black's fifth move is shown in Figure 5.17. Does the position in Figure 5.17 match what you visualized or played out on your board? If so, good job!

Appendix A

CHESS TEST

The chess test measures students' chess knowledge. Students answer on a separate piece of notebook paper so that you can reuse your photocopies of the chess test. Have the students write a different letter of the alphabet (from A through P) on each line of notebook paper. Exception: Leave two lines instead of one line for answers G and I. Students will write their answers to the right of each letter. Figure A.1 shows a nine-year-old student taking the chess test.

Figure A.1.
Taking the Chess Test.

Here are the symbols, words, and abbreviations for the chess test.

Symbols	Words	Abbreviations
♔, ♚	white king, black king	K
♕, ♛	white queen; black queen	Q
♖, ♜	white rook, black rook	R
♗, ♝	white bishop, black bishop	B
♘, ♞	white knight, black knight	N
♙, ♟	white pawn, black pawn	P

A. Write the abbreviation of the piece in Diagram #1.

B. Write the abbreviations of the mystery **two** pieces that could be in Diagram #2.

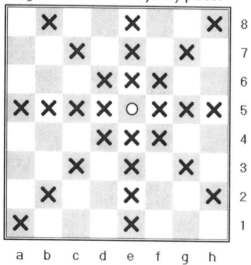

Diagram #1: O is the mystery piece.

Xs are legal moves on this turn.

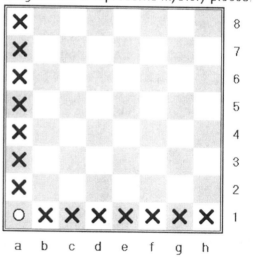

Diagram #2: O represents mystery pieces.

X's are legal moves on this turn.

From *Science, Math, Checkmate: 32 Chess Activities for Inquiry and Problem Solving* by Alexey W. Root. Westport, CT: Teacher Ideas Press. Copyright © 2008.

C. Write the abbreviations of the **two** pieces that could be in Diagram #3.

Diagram #3: O represents mystery pieces.

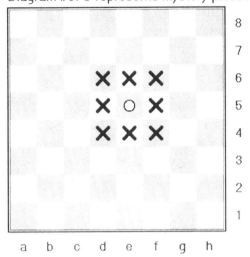

X's are legal moves on this turn.

D. Write the abbreviations of the **three** pieces or pawns that could be in Diagram #4.

Diagram #4: O represents mystery pieces.

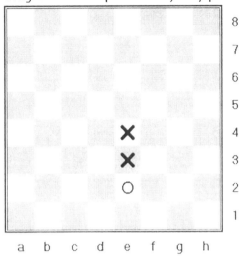

X's are legal moves on this turn.

E. Write the abbreviation of the mystery piece in Diagram #5.

Diagram #5: O is the mystery piece.

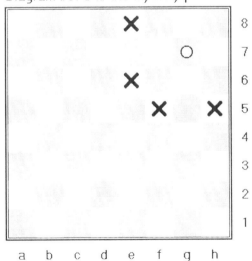

X's are legal moves on this turn.

F. Write the abbreviations of the **two** pieces that could be in Diagram #6.

Diagram #6: O represents mystery pieces

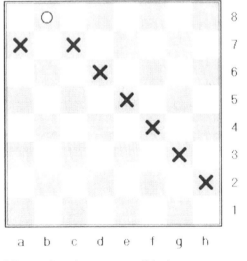

X's are legal moves on this turn.

From *Science, Math, Checkmate: 32 Chess Activities for Inquiry and Problem Solving* by Alexey W. Root. Westport, CT: Teacher Ideas Press. Copyright © 2008.

G. Which chess diagram (#1 or #2 below) represents the correct way to set up the chess pieces? Give two reasons for your answer.

Diagram #1

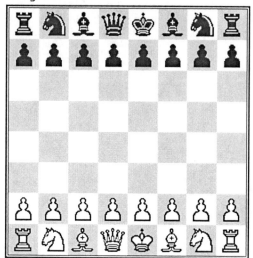

Diagram #2

H. One pawn = one point. How many points is the Q worth?

I. What is stalemate?

J. What is the symbol for check in algebraic notation?

K. Which of the following prevents castling?

    a. Your king has moved.

    b. The rook you want to castle with has moved.

    c. You are in check.

    d. All of the choices a, b, and c.

L. What is the notation for queenside castling?

M.

White has just played 1. b2–b4.

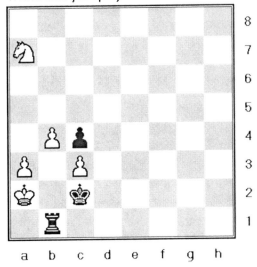

What is black's best response?

N.

Black to move and checkmate this move.

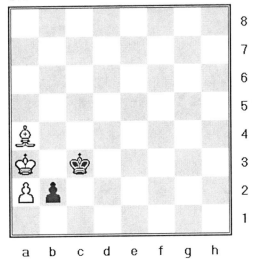

Write the checkmate in notation.

O.

What is the name of Black's opening?

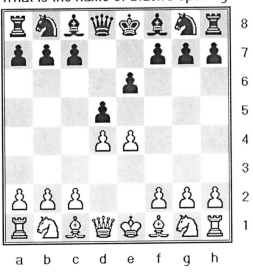

a) English b) Sicilian or c) French

P.

Black to move.

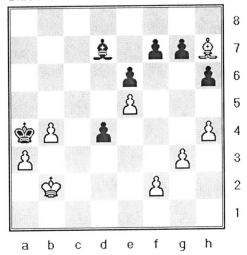

If 1....Bb5, what is white's best response?

Figure A.2.
Chess Test.

From *Science, Math, Checkmate: 32 Chess Activities for Inquiry and Problem Solving* by Alexey W. Root. Westport, CT: Teacher Ideas Press. Copyright © 2008.

This chess test may be given at the start of chess instruction as a pre-test and/or given after chess instruction as a post-test. To shorten the test for younger students, administer it in two or three parts.

Answer Key for Chess Test

The correct answers for the Chess Test are provided in this section. You decide how much weight to give each correct answer. Students with more correct answers will comprehend the chess content of the 32 activities in *Science, Math, Checkmate* faster than their fellow students. In the test, questions A–H are at the pawn level; questions I and J are at the knight level; questions K and L are at the bishop level; questions M and N are at the rook level; and question O is at the queen level; and question P is at the king level.

Answers:

Question A: Q.
Question B: R, Q.
Question C: K, Q.
Question D: P, R, Q.
Question E: N.
Question F: B, Q.
Question G: Diagram #1 is correct. Each player must start with a white square where his or her right hand is. Also, the queen must start on her own color.
Question H: 9 points.
Question I: Stalemate is when a king is not in check but there are no legal moves for his side. It is scored as a draw.
Question J: +.
Question K: d. All of the choices a, b, and c.
Question L: 0-0-0.
Question M: cxb3 e.p.#. I was inspired to create this position from one of the problems in *Beginning Chess* (Pandolfini, 1993).
Question N: b1(N)#.
Question O: c. French.
Question P: Bc2#. Background: This position occurred in a game of mine (March 3, 2007, Round 1, Denton Open). Black played 1....Bb5 and offered me a draw. Black planned to promote his passed d-pawn. If I moved my king to stop the d-pawn, then his king would take my a- and b-pawns. I declined the draw offer and played 2. Bc2#.

Appendix B

ANSWER KEY FOR ACTIVITIES

Chapter 2: Scientific Inquiry

Physical Properties of Pieces: Sample answer key is given in Figure B.1. Actual student answers will vary depending on the materials used to make the sets.

Pawn Game: Answers will vary depending on students' results in the pawn game trials.

3-on-3: Fine (1941, p. 45) gives the following solutions: 1. b6 cxb6 2. a6 bxa6 3. c6 [and the c-pawn promotes or] 1. b6 axb6 2. c6 bxc6 3. a6 [and the a-pawn promotes]. If the students have not found these solutions, show them on the demonstration board. Encourage students to notice that white's sacrifice of two pawns allowed his third and final pawn to become passed and promote. Note that 1. a6 does not create a passed pawn, because black plays 1....b6 2. cxb6 cxb6 and the pawns are locked. Similarly, 1. c6 fails to 1....b6 2. axb6 axb6.

20 Questions: Answers will vary depending on the mystery piece or pawn chosen.

Black Box: Answers will vary depending on where students place the king.

Computers and Checkmates: The pattern for checkmating with a king and queen against a lone king can be found in the software, Web sites, and books listed within the materials section of the activity.

Name *Answer Key (sample)*   Date_____

PHYSICAL PROPERTIES CHART

Directions: Check off or complete each chart entry that applies to each piece in your group's bag.

My group had bag number _____.

Piece Number	clear	opaque	shiny	dull	color	Weight	Float	Sink	Magnet Attracts
1 (metal)		x	x		silver			x	Yes
2 (wood)		x		x	cream		x		No
3 (stone)		x		x	green			x	No
4 (glass)	x		x		clear			x	No
5 (plastic)		x		x	black		x		No
6 (clay)		x		x	red			x	No

After observing the six pieces this is my conclusion:

Piece 1 is made out of metal, which is a nonrenewable resource.

Piece 2 is made out of wood, which is a renewable resource.

Piece 3 is made out of stone, which is a nonrenewable resource.

Piece 4 is made out of glass, which is a nonrenewable resource.

Piece 5 is made out of plastic, which is a nonrenewable resource.

Piece 6 is made out of clay, which is a nonrenewable resource.

Figure B.1.
Sample answers for Physical Properties Chart.

From *Science, Math, Checkmate: 32 Chess Activities for Inquiry and Problem Solving* by Alexey W. Root. Westport, CT: Teacher Ideas Press. Copyright © 2008.

To e.p. or not to e.p.: Here is the answer key for Figure 2.9. Comments in brackets are for clarification, but are not required in the students' answers. Diagram #1: 1....bxc3 e.p. Diagram #2: 2. hxg6 e.p. Diagram #3: Yes, the diagram is accurate. (Explanation: The g5 pawn is removed when the e.p. capture is made. The capturing pawn ends up on g6.) Diagram #4: No, black cannot take e.p. En passant captures must be made immediately after the opponent's pawn double-jumps on the adjacent file. (Note: Since intervening moves have been played, the c4 pawn is no longer vulnerable to an e.p. capture.)

Criteria Challenge: There are several solutions that meet each challenge. Here are solutions created by rising fourth through eighth-grade students enrolled in the second week of the M.O.S.A.I.C. chess course (June 18–22, 2007). Without prompting from me, the five groups selected different challenges from each other. For challenge one: White: Kf3, Qe4; Black Kd5, Rd6, Rc5. The second group that selected challenge one came up with: White: Kf2, Qh3; Black: Kh1, Rg6, Re7. For challenge two: White Kh5, Bf6; Black: Kh7, Bg8, Pf7. For challenge three, two rising sixth graders created a position with unlikely features such as many pieces **en prise** and two light-squared bishops for White. Their classmates voted for their position. Here is a simplified version of it: White: Kd1, Bg2, Na6, Nf5, Rf8, Ps a3, b2, c2, d5, h3. Black: Kd7, Na2, Ng5, Rh5, Bh2, Ps a7, c5, e6, g7, h7. Black has just played c7-c5, and White plays dxc6 e.p.#. For challenge four: White: Kf1, Nf2; Black: Kh1, Ph2.

Chess Models: The solution for Figure 2.11 is 1....fxg3#. The solution for Figure 2.12 is 1....Qg3+ 2. Rxg3 fxg3#.

The Good Bishop: Answers for Figure 2.13 are Diagram 1: (B). **Bf7** to win the pawns. Diagram 2: (A). **Bh4** Eliminating the knight from the game. Diagram 3: (C). **h5** Locking the pawn on h6, followed by **Bg7**, winning the h-pawn. Diagram 4: (B) The white bishop attacks the black pawn chain, planning a capture on a7 next move. Black, to move, cannot defend his pawns. And if **1....Nxb5 2. cxb5 c4 3. Be5** stops the promotion plans of the c-pawn.

Stalemate Surprise: The K & P vs. K & Q position ending is drawn if the pawn, which is one square from promoting, is a bishop's pawn or a rook's pawn. The method for drawing is for the defender (the side with the king and pawn) to stalemate himself. With the bishop's pawn (c- or f-pawn), the stalemate method is to sacrifice one's pawn on the second (if black) or seventh (if white) rank to the enemy queen when the defending king is in the corner. If the queen takes the pawn, the defending king is stalemated. This position is shown in Diagram One of Figure B.2. If the queen refuses to take the pawn, she has nothing better to do than to give **perpetual check.** With the rook's pawn (a- or h-pawn), stalemate is accomplished by the defending king placing himself in front of his own pawn and having no remaining moves, as shown in Diagram Two in Figure B.2.

The king and queen will checkmate a king paired with a g-, d-, e-, or b-pawn. The method, shown in Diagrams Three and Four in Figure B.2,

Diagram One

Black to move.

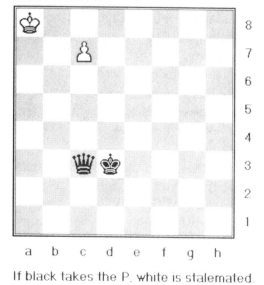

If black takes the P. white is stalemated.

Diagram Two

Black to move.

Stalemate: Black has no legal moves.

Diagram Three

Black's move. If 1....Kf1 2. Qxd2

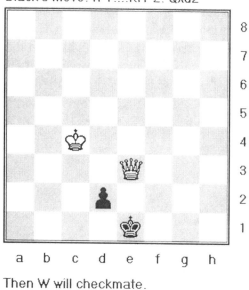

Then W will checkmate.

Diagram Four

Black's move. If 1....Ka6 2. Ka8 Qxb7#

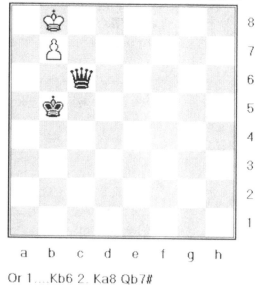

Or 1....Kb6 2. Ka8 Qb7#

Figure B.2.
Answer key for Stalemate Surprise.

is for the queen to check the defending king until he either gives up his pawn or blocks his own pawn from promoting. In Diagram Three, black surrenders his pawn and will lose to the K and Q vs. K checkmate. In Diagram Four, where the king has been driven in front of his own pawn, the attacking king moves closer to him. The game ends with the pawn being captured and the defending king succumbing to a king and queen checkmate. These K & Q vs. K & P positions are explained in Fine (1941, pp. 522–524).

Chapter 3: Mathematical Problem Solving

Covering the Board: Rooks: According to Watkins (2004, p. 99), there are 33,514,312 ways that eight rooks can cover all the squares of an 8-by-8 board. One answer is to place rooks on a1, b1, c1, d1, e1, f1, g1, and h1.

Perimeter and Surface Area of the Board: Answers for Figure 3.3: perimeter of the board: 8 x 4 = 32 units; surface area of the board: 8 x 8 = 64 square units.

Covering the Board: Kings: Answers are within the activity.

Eight Queens: One solution is Qs on a2, b4, c6, d8, e3, f1, g7, and h5.

Balancing Chess Equations: Equations will vary based on how students combine the chess pawns and pieces.

Pawns, Pieces, Proportions, and Probability: Figure 3.12 answers will vary depending on which pieces and pawns were selected from the chess bag by students. Figure 3.13 answers: For the knight (N), bishop (B), and (R): Column 2 = 4, Column 3 = 32, Column 4 = 4/32, Column 5 = 1/8, Column 6 = .125 or 12.5%. For the queen (Q) and king (K): Column 2 = 2; Column 3 = 32; Column 4 = 2/32; Column 5 = 1/16; Column 6 = .0625 or 6.25%.

Practice Producing Polygons: Answers to Figure 3.15 will vary based on the polygons chosen by each student.

Chess Players' Stats: Figure 3.18 U.S. Open crosstable worksheet answers: 1. Round 6 2a. Felecan scored 7 points (of 9 rounds) 2b. Using William's method, 77% (7 x 11 = 77). 2c. Actual percentage, 7 divided by 9, is .$\overline{7}$ or, rounded, 78%. 3a. Shulman scored 8 points (of 9 rounds). 3b. Using William's method, 88% (8 x 11 = 88). 3c. Actual percentage, 8 divided by 9, is .$\overline{8}$ or (rounded) 89%.

Pick a Pocketful of Pieces: Answer is 1/10 or 10%. Here are a couple of solutions, created by my daughter Clarissa when she was a first-semester ninth grader. I reproduce her answers in some detail here, because from such detail one can determine if a student understands the mathematical concepts behind the calculations. I asked Clarissa to solve the same question listed in the activity's procedure, "What is the probability that the values of three chess pieces taken from a pocket would add up to seven?" Clarissa quickly decided that B + N + P = 7, but that no other combination of three figures added up to seven.

The probability calculation was harder for her. Her first fraction try (1/5 x 1/4 x 1/3 = 1/60) was a mathematically balanced equation but one that misrepresented the probability. Her second equation (3/5 x 1/2 x 1/3 = 1/10) was correct. (Note that she could have used decimals to represent these probabilities: .6 x .5 x $.\overline{3}$ = $.0\overline{9}$, which rounds to .10.) Clarissa explained the reasoning behind her equation: "When I pick the first piece, I have three chances out of five to get one of the three figures (P, B, or N) that I need. When I choose the second piece, there are four figures left. Two of them are ones that I need, which is 2/4 or 1/2. Then there are three figures left in the pocket, only one of which will be the one that I need to complete the B + N + P combination. I multiply all the probabilities together to get the answer." I then asked Clarissa to prove that her answer (1/10) was correct. She started to make a chart to prove her solution, but then decided to draw a tree diagram. She had learned to draw a tree diagram in middle school. For tree diagrams, see page 255 of NCTM, 2000.

Her chart started like this:

RQN

RNQ

And then she drew a tree diagram, of which I reproduce just the bishop's tree in Figure B.3. When Clarissa finished drawing all five trees (B, N, P, Q, and R), she highlighted the branches that corresponded to B + N + P (in any order). Each of her five trees had 12 branches. Of those

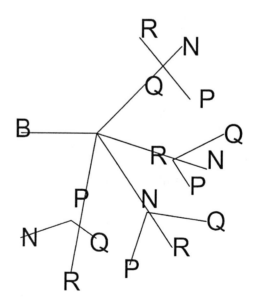

Figure B.3.
Tree diagram.

60 total branches, six had the following forms: B-N-P, B-P-N, N-B-P, N-P-B, P-B-N, and P-N-B. Those six branches comprised 1/10 of the total branches of all the trees, confirming Clarissa's fractional calculation.

Mazes and Monsters: For the bishop maze in Figure 3.19: 1. Bxc5, 2. Bxd6, 3. Bxe7, 4. Bxf6, 5. Bxe5, 6. Bxf4, 7. Bxg3, 8. Bxf2, 9. Bxe3, 10. Bxd2, 11. Bxc3. For the rook maze in Figure 3.19: 1. Rxc2, 2. Rxc4, 3. Rxc8, 4. Rxe8, 5. Rxe3, 6. Rxh3, 7. Rxh6, 8. Rxh7, 9. Rxb7, 10. Rxa7, 11. Rxa6, 12. Rxb6.

Working Backward: The pattern for the K + Q + R vs. K checkmate is shown within the activity.

Transforming Figures: The answers for Figure 3.25 are as follows. The answer for preimage 1 is: White Qd3, white Ke3, white Rd2, white Bf1; black Ke1, black Bd1, black Pf2, and black Nf3. The mate in one is 1. Rxd1#. The answer for preimage 2 is: White Bb8, white Pc7, white Ne8, white Rf8, white Ke7; black Kc8, black Nd8, black Pd6. The mate in one is 1. Nxd6#.

Chapter 4: Interdisciplinary

Learning Chess Pieces: Names of the chess figures, spelled correctly, followed by their diagram symbols (white version): king (♔), queen (♕), rook (♖), bishop (♗), knight (♘), pawn (♙). Correct starting position of a board is shown in Figure B.4.

Map My School on a Board: Answers to Figure 4.1 will vary based on the rooms and route selected by the students.

The Knights Can't Wait!: According to the story, Coco is slower than Grandma since she leaves earlier but arrives later. If the extension (step six) is attempted, discuss why it always takes an odd number of moves for a knight to travel from a white square to a black square (Coco) or from a black square to a white square (Grandma). For example, with (white) Coco starting on b1 and (black) Grandma starting on b8: 1. Nc3 Nc6 2. Nd5 Nb4 3. Ne7 Na2 4. Nc6 Nc3 5. Nb8 Nb1.

Gifted students might try to meet the story requirements exactly, as my 10-year-old son William did. William spent 30 minutes fruitlessly attempting for Coco knight to start a half-move earlier but finish a half-move later than Grandma knight. He even changed the starting squares of the knights to same-color squares to see if the story requirements could be met. But knights take an even number of moves to get to squares of the same color. William concluded, "The problem is that not every number is even. There are some odd numbers. You need Coco to take one more

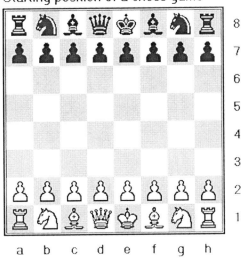

Starting position of a chess game

White Q starts on d1; black Q on d8

Figure B.4.
Starting position of a chess game.

move than Grandma. Grandma, for example, needs to get there in two. And Coco needs to get there in three. No matter where you place them on the board, they can't do that."

Then William spent another 15 minutes figuring out what pieces or pawns would meet the story requirements, "It would work with bishops, for example a white bishop on b1 and a black bishop on c8. 1. Bf5 Bd7 2. Bh3 Bf5 3. Bg4 Bb1 4. Bc8. But it would not work if Coco is a white-squared bishop and Grandma is a dark-squared bishop. It works with rooks, kings, and queens too, but not with knights and pawns. It also works if Coco and Grandma are different types of pieces or pawns. It would be best if Coco was a pawn and Grandma was a knight, because then it would be challenging for students but it can be done. For example, a white Coco pawn starts on e2 and a black Grandma knight is on e6. 1. e4 Nf4 2. e5 Ne2 3. e6."

The King's Chessboard: The solution is shown within the activity.

How to Castle: The rising fourth through eighth-grade students enrolled in the second week of the M.O.S.A.I.C. chess course (June 18–22, 2007) wrote essays that included the five topics covered in the activity: (1) Why it is good to castle; (2) How to castle kingside; (3) How to castle queenside; (4) Conditions that permit castling; and (5) Conditions that prohibit castling. Figures B.5, B.6, and B.7 are from rising fifth-grade student Mehul Gore. His excellent homework serves as a model answer. Figure B.8 is a photo of Mehul.

Kasparov versus the World: Answers vary depending on the moves played by each classroom.

Know More, Move More!: Answers vary depending on the review questions.

Move Order Mystery: Opening Line One moves (in order): 1. e4 e5 2. Nf3 Nf6 3. Nxe5 Nxe4 4. Qe2 Nf6 5. Nc6+ resigns. Opening Line Two moves (in order): 1. e4 e5 2. Nf3 Nf6 3. Nxe5 d6 4. Nf3 Nxe4 5. Qe2 Qe7

Openings around the World: Here are 10 moves for students to memorize from the Sicilian Defense, Dragon variation. An excellent explanation of each move can be found in Wolff (2005, pp. 167–171). 1. e4 c5 2. Nf3 d6 3. d4 cxd4 4. Nxd4 Nf6 5. Nc3 g6 6. Be2 Bg7 7. 0–0 0–0 8. Be3 Nc6 9. Nb3 Be6 10. f4.

Why Castle?/Introduction

Castling is a good way to help your rook and King. First of all, why should you castle? You castle because you can get your rook in the game or you can use it for king safety.

How to castle

If you are doing a kingside castle, move the King 2 squares to the right. Move your rook 2 squares to the left. The King should be on the g file and the rook should be on the f file. The symbol/notation for a kingside castle is 0-0. If you are doing a queenside castle, move the King 2 squares to the left. Move the rook 3 spaces to the right. The King should be on the c file and the rook should be on the d file. The symbol/notation for a queenside castle is 0-0-0. A queenside castle has nothing to do with a queen. It is named queenside castle because you are castling from the queen's side.

Figure B.5.
How to Castle, page one.

Conditions that permit castling

Here are some ways you
can castle the right way!
- You can't move the king or
  it rook in the whole game
- There has to be empty squares
  between the king and the rook

Conditions that prohibit castling

Castling might be cool but there
are some disadvantages......

- If you are in check you
  can't castle

- You can't castle in or over
  check

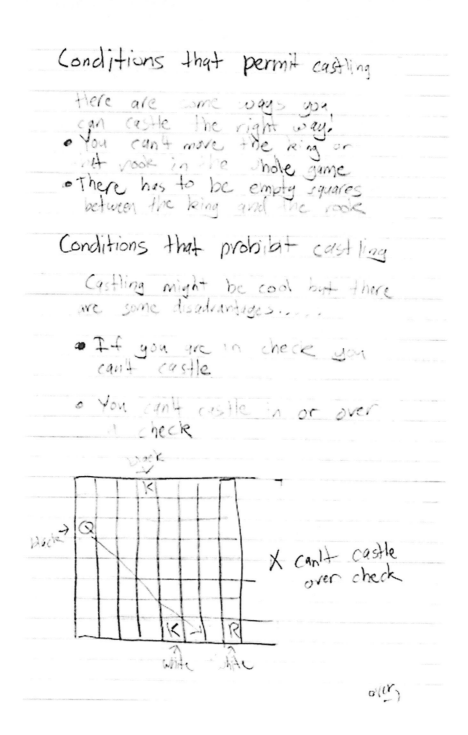

X can't castle
over check

Figure B.6.
How to Castle, page two.

From *Science, Math, Checkmate: 32 Chess Activities for Inquiry and Problem Solving* by Alexey W. Root.
Westport, CT: Teacher Ideas Press. Copyright © 2008.

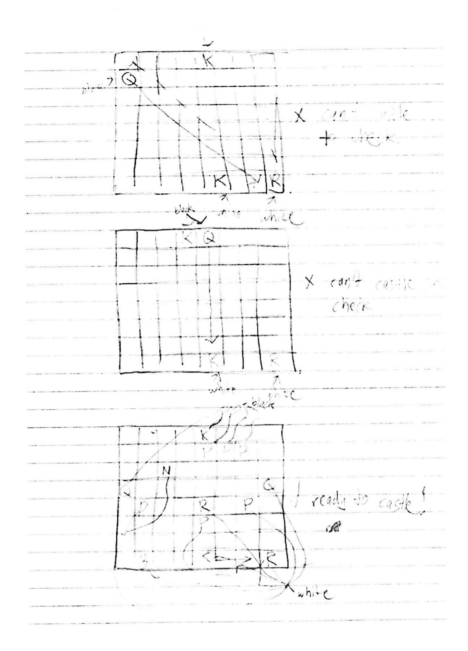

Figure B.7.
How to Castle, page three.

Figure B.8.
Mehul Gore, castling essay author.

Chapter 5: Chess Basics

Check, Checkmate, or Stalemate? (Figure 5.11): Diagram 1 is a checkmate. The black king is in check and cannot take the checking piece, block the check, or move to a safe square. This particular mate is called the one-rook checkmate. Diagram 2 is a stalemate. The white queen limits all of the black king's moves, and black has no other piece or pawn to move. Diagram 3 is a check. The white king can escape the black knight's check by moving to d3 or c4. Diagram 4 is a checkmate. The white king is in check and cannot take the checking piece, block the check, or move to a safe square. This particular mate is called the two-bishop checkmate.

Appendix C

REVIEW OF KASPAROV AND POLGAR CURRICULA

In 2006, world champions Kasparov and Polgar published classroom chess curricula. In this book review, the Kasparov Chess Foundation curriculum (Khmelnitsky, Khodarkovsky, & Zadorozny, 2006) is abbreviated as Khmelnitsky et al. and the Polgar Chess Foundation curriculum (Polgar, 2006) is abbreviated as Polgar. Khmelnitsky et al. divides introductory chess into 40 lessons (Book 1) and Polgar has 30 lessons. The similarities between Book 1 of Khmelnitsky et al. and the entire Polgar are striking and comprise the main focus of this review. The differences, covered in the next two paragraphs, stem largely from formatting and from the greater page length of Khmelnitsky et al.

Khmelnitsky et al. has more appealing graphics and design than the Polgar's PDF document. Each Khmelnitsky et al. book has an attractive color cover with cartoon illustrations. Inside, there are large chess diagrams, easy-to-read print, cartoons, and photos. Books 2 and 3 of Khmelnitsky et al. provide content not covered by Polgar: Book 3 is a chess coloring book. Book 2's pages could be photocopied for classroom worksheets or for homework. Though Book 2 generally provides practice of the piece or concept learned that day in Book 1, sometimes Book 2 uses terms, such as "targets of attack" (Book 2, p. 29), not found in Book 1. The Khmelnitsky et al. books might be slow in arriving. I mailed my order form and check for $59.90 on November 16, 2006, but didn't receive my books until January 9, 2007.

In contrast, Polgar can be ordered and received in one day, via e-mail. Without coloring books or worksheets, Polgar is a compact document. The diagrams and print are readable. Several of the pages have enlarged, decorative chess pieces or chess cartoons. There aren't any photos. One final major difference is that Khmelnitsky et al. Book 1 gives scripts to teachers about what to say while demonstrating each chess position. Polgar is not scripted, so the teacher must translate the chess concepts into child-friendly language. For example, regarding a pawn ending on page 37, Polgar states, "In this position, it is critical who is to move. In this case, it is not a pleasure to have the obligation to move."

Despite the differences mentioned above, Book 1 of Khmelnitsky et al. and Polgar have comparable chess content presented in almost the same order. The history of chess and how to label the squares with algebraic notation comprise the first two lessons of Khmelnitsky et al. and the first lesson of Polgar. Neither curriculum guides teachers about chess equipment purchases. Teachers might be confused about what boards to use by this sentence from Khmelnitsky et al., "Most chess boards that are available for sale do not have lettering and numbers" (p. 13). Polgar doesn't comment about chess equipment, and never uses the term *demonstration board*. The omissions of chess equipment requirements and of ordering information are curious because the lessons in Khmelnitsky et al. and Polgar require chess sets, boards, and a demonstration board.

Lessons 4 and 5 (Khmelnitsky et al.) and lesson 2 (Polgar) teach the rules of pawn movement. Polgar includes en passant here, while Khmelnitsky et al. doesn't teach en passant until lesson 19. The Pawn Game (Khmelnitsky et al.) or Pawn War (Polgar) is also introduced, where students play with eight pawns versus eight pawns. The next piece for Khmelnitsky et al. and Polgar is the rook. After the scripted lecture on the rook's movements, Khmelnitsky et al. asks students to play the Pawn Game with rooks also added to that game. In contrast, Polgar introduces chess mazes. In mazes, the pawns are stationary and the piece (in this case the rook) moves around to capture each pawn. Polgar also recommends a game where one student has a rook and the other has six pawns, to be played until: (1) the first pawn promotes, or (2) the rook captures of all the pawns, or (3) 20 moves elapse.

The bishop is next for both Khmelnitsky et al. and Polgar. Khmelnitsky et al. continues the pattern of teacher lecture about the bishop's movements followed by a Pawn Game (with rooks and bishops also added). Polgar likewise explains the bishop's moves and asks students to complete a bishop chess maze. The Polgar practice game pits a student with two bishops versus one with two rooks, and the next lesson has a lone bishop combat three pawns.

The queen is next for Khmelnitsky et al. (lesson 8) and Polgar (lesson 6). Once again, Khmelnitsky et al. students play the Pawn Game (now with rooks, bishops, and queens) and Polgar students play a queen maze. The eight-queens problem makes an appearance in Book 2 of

Khmelnitsky et al. and also in Polgar. Lesson 9 (Khmelnitsky et al.) and lesson 8 (Polgar) introduce the knight, with Khmelnitsky et al. concluding the lesson with a Pawn Game (with rooks, bishops, knights, and queens). Polgar asks students to attempt a knight's tour ("Try to jump with the Knight from one square to another covering *all* 64 squares on the chess board," Polgar, p. 17, italics in original). The next topics are the king, check, and checkmate (lesson 10, Khmelnitsky et al.; lesson 9, Polgar). In Khmelnitsky et al. students now play a real chess game, as all the pieces have been added to the Pawn Game. In Khmelnitsky et al. lessons 11–15, students learn some basic mates (such as the two-rook mate) and stalemate. Polgar students, in lessons 9–11, practice problems that require either checkmate or stalemate in one. Both Khmelnitsky et al. and Polgar also teach how to mate with a king and queen against a lone king during these lesson plans.

Having covered the pieces in the first halves of Khmelnitsky et al. and Polgar, the curricula proceed to topics of development, notation, and tactics. First the rules of development and opening principles are introduced. Then both Khmelnitsky et al. and Polgar teach algebraic notation, with Khmelnitsky et al. giving the long version first (starting square to ending square, i.e., 1. e2-e4) and Polgar showing just the short version (ending square only, i.e., 1. e4). Short games or game fragments—showing good and poor opening play, including opening traps and quick checkmates—are featured in seven lessons in Khmelnitsky et al. and four lessons in Polgar. In the final one-third of both Khmelnitsky et al. and Polgar, topics include the following tactics: **forks,** pins, **removing the guard,** and **skewers.**

Although the majority of pages in both Khmelnitsky et al. and Polgar are solely concerned with chess content, both curricula briefly cite educational connections. Kasparov's introduction to Khmelnitsky et al. states, "No one has ever doubted the positive effects of chess on the mind" (p. 6). And Khmelnitsky et al.'s Book 1 has six pages of "Bloom's Taxonomy of Educational Objectives Applied to Chess Learning in the Classroom" written by Pete Tamburro. Polgar's lesson 1 suggests that teachers might assign research questions about India and Persia. Polgar's lesson 1 also compares algebraic notation to map-reading. Other Polgar lessons don't offer academic objectives. With less than 3% of Khmelnitsky et al. and Polgar devoted to connecting chess content and academic objectives, school administrators might be skeptical about adopting these curricula. Nevertheless, classroom teachers or after-school program instructors with the desire to teach chess are likely to welcome Khmelnitsky et al. and Polgar as useful lesson plans for communicating chess content.

Glossary

Algebraic notation is the most common notation system for writing chess moves. Each square has a name based on its file (a–h) and rank (1–8) coordinates. An older system of notation is descriptive notation, which is based on the names and squares that pieces occupy at the beginning of the game, that is, 1. Kt.-KB3 means knight to king's bishop's three. In algebraic, that same move would be written 1. Nf3. Chapter 5, "Chess Basics," reviews the symbols of algebraic notation.

Attacking describes "a move or series of moves to mate, gain material, or obtain advantage. It also means to make or threaten such moves" (Pandolfini, 1995, p. 32).

Bishop (B) is worth three pawns, according to most sources. Each side begins the game with one bishop that moves along the light squares, and one that moves along the dark squares. A bishop moves diagonally, as many squares as are not blocked by its own pieces. It can capture an enemy piece or pawn that is in its path.

Board is the arena for the chess game and is short for chessboard. The board has 32 light squares and 32 dark squares in an alternating pattern, arranged in eight vertical columns and eight horizontal rows. For chess teaching, acquire boards with algebraic notation marked on the borders.

Bughouse is a variant of chess. The game is played by two teams of two partners each. One partner plays white and the other partner plays black on two adjacent boards. As captures are made, the partners hand each other captured pieces and pawns. When on move, a player either moves a chess figure already on the board or drops one pawn or piece (previously given to them by their partner) into an unoccupied square. When one person on a team wins, the entire team wins. For all the rules, visit http://www.chessvariants.com/multiplayer.dir/tandem.html.

Captures occur when a pawn or piece moves to a square occupied by an enemy pawn or piece. The capture removes the enemy piece or pawn from the board.

Castling is a move notated 0-0 (kingside castling, "castling short") or 0-0-0 (queenside castling, "castling long"). Castling can be done once per side, per game, if the king and rook that want to castle with each other haven't moved previously and the king is not in check, crossing over a checked square, or ending up on a checked square. Also, there can be no pieces between the king and rook during the castling move. To castle, the king moves two squares toward its rook, and the rook hops over the king and lands on the square horizontally adjacent to the king.

Center of the board includes the squares e4, d4, e5, and d5.

Check (+) is a direct attack on a king by an enemy piece or pawn. The king must get out of check by capturing the checking piece or pawn, blocking the check with one of his own men, or moving to a square that is not attacked.

Checkmate (++ or # or mate) is when the king is in check and cannot escape from check. Being checkmated means that one has lost the chess game.

Chess is a two-player board game of strategy.

Chess club is a gathering of chess players for instruction, casual chess play, or tournaments. Most cities and many schools have chess clubs; find club listings at the USCF Web site. There is even an Internet Chess Club, http://www.chessclub.com, with 30,000 members worldwide.

Chess in Education Certificate online courses have been offered by the University of Texas at Dallas since the fall of 2001. The courses are available nationally, via the Internet. For course information, search for "Chess in Education Certificate" at the UT TeleCampus http://www.telecampus.utsystem.edu/.

Chessmen are the "pieces and pawns considered as a group" (Pandolfini, 1995, p. 66).

Clocks are used to time chess games. One's time runs when it is one's move. At the completion of one's move one punches a button to start one's opponent's clock running. Some games use sudden death (SD) time controls. That is, one must finish one's whole game before the time elapses. Common SD time controls include G/5 (game in five minutes per player, i.e., 10 minutes maximum game time, called speed chess) and G/30 (game in thirty minutes per player, called action chess). G/30 is the fastest time control allowed for a game to be rated under the regular rating system by USCF; G/5-G/29 are rated under a separate quick chess rating system.

In contrast, some tournaments use traditional time controls such as 40/2, 20/1, 20/1: make 40 moves before your first two hours elapse, then make 20 moves per hour for the next two time controls. For both SD and traditional time controls, a loss on time (a flag fall) means a loss of the game, except when the side "winning on time" doesn't have sufficient material to deliver a checkmate (i.e., only has a K and B, or only has a K and a N), *see* draw.

Covering means to attack squares with your pieces. For example, a queen in the center of an open board covers 27 squares.

Crosstable is a post-event record of a chess tournament. The crosstable lists players by score, from highest to lowest. The crosstable also shows which opponent each player faced in each round.

Defense is "a move or series of moves designed to meet opposing threats and attacks, whether immediate or long range. In the openings, a defense is a system of play whose characteristic positions are determined largely by Black" (Pandolfini, 1995, p. 88).

Demonstration board (demo board) is a large, upright chess board that either hangs from a nail or map hook or is mounted on an easel. Its chessmen are held on magnetically or fit into slots. The demonstration board is used for showing chess moves to groups of students. One can order demonstration boards from most chess retailers, including from USCF.

Developing pieces properly in the opening involves moving them from their starting squares to squares that attack the center of the board or other important targets.

Diagonal is "a slanted row of same-colored squares. There are 26 different diagonals on the chessboard" (Pandolfini, 1995, p. 90).

Diagram is a two-dimensional representation of a chess position. Traditionally, the white chessmen start at the bottom of a chess diagram. One can make diagrams by hand, by abbreviating the chessmen's names (K, Q, R, B, N, and P) and circling the black chessmen. Or one can use a software program such as DiagTransfer, http://alain.blaisot.free.fr/DiagTransfer/English/home.htm, which includes fonts that give figurine representations of white and black pieces.

Discovered check is "the movement of a piece or pawn that results in a check by an unmoved piece" (Eade, 2005, p. 320).

Draws are scored as a half a point for each player. As Eade (2005, p. 321) wrote, there are several ways for a draw to result "(a) by agreement of both players, (b) by stalemate, (c) by the declaration and proof of one player that the same position has appeared three times (with the same player to move), (d) by the declaration and proof of one player that there have been 50 moves during which no piece has been taken and no pawns have been moved, although there are some exceptions to the 50 move rule." If one's opponent runs out of time (*see* clock)—but one doesn't have sufficient material to checkmate— a draw is declared. Finally, in some cases, tournament directors may adjudicate games as draws, wins, or losses, usually when there is a time constraint to complete a club game or a team match.

Endgame (ending) is the stage of the game where there are few chess pieces and pawns left on the board. Often the king becomes active, attacking enemy pawns and supporting his own pawn's promotion. Figure gloss.1 shows students contemplating an endgame position.

Figure gloss.1.
Playing an endgame.

En passant (e.p.) is French for *in passing.* The en passant capture can be executed by pawns which are on one's own fifth rank (i.e., rank 5 for white pawns, rank 4 for black pawns) when an enemy pawn does a double jump to the square adjacent to them. Then the fifth-rank pawn can capture the enemy pawn as if it had only moved one square. The en passant capture is optional, and if chosen must be done on the half-move immediately following the enemy pawn's double jump.

En prise, a French term *in take,* means to leave (or to move) a piece or a pawn to a square where it can be captured for free.

Fédération Internationale des Échecs (FIDE) is the world chess federation with 161 countries (including the United States represented by USCF) as members. FIDE maintains a rating system, awards international titles (GM, IM, etc.), and has organized world championships. Web site http://www.fide.com.

Fianchetto is an Italian word meaning *little flank* and is pronounced "fee-an-ket-to" (Wolff, 2005, p. 169). Fianchettoed bishops on g2 or b2 for white and g7 or b7 for black attack the center squares along the longest diagonals.

Files are the vertical columns of squares on the board. There are 8 files, labeled a, b, c, d, e, f, g, and h.

Forks are simultaneous attacks on two or more pawns or pieces.

Grandmaster (GM) is an international title awarded by FIDE to players who perform above a predetermined level (usually above 2500 FIDE rating) at tournaments with other titled players. Usually it takes three such performances (three norms) to get the GM title.

Heuristics are problem-solving strategies, specifically rules of thumb derived by experience. One uses heuristics when there isn't a preestablished formula or algorithm for solving a problem. An example is: Understand the problem, make a plan, carry out the plan, and evaluate the solution for reasonableness.

Illegal move is one prohibited by the rules of chess. When noticed before the end of the game, it causes the position to be reset to just before the illegal move. At that point, a legal move must be played instead.

International Master (IM) is a title awarded by FIDE to players who have performed at a specified level (usually above 2400 FIDE rating) at three international tournaments with other titled players.

King (K) is able to move one square in any direction. The king captures the same way that it moves. When the king is checkmated or stalemated, the game is over. *See also* castling.

Kingside is the half of the board that includes the e-, f-, g-, and h-files.

Knight (N) is the piece that looks (on most chess sets) like a horse. Like a horse, it can jump over pieces and pawns. The knight's move is in the shape of capital L. Or the knight's move can be described as two squares horizontally followed by one square vertically, or two squares vertically followed by one square horizontally. It can capture an enemy piece if it lands on the square of that piece. The knight is generally said to be worth three pawns.

Legal move is a move made in accordance with the rules of chess.

Losses can occur because of checkmate, a loss on time (*see* clock), or because of resigning. A loss is scored as a zero.

Masters possess a USCF rating between 2200 and 2400. Players with ratings above 2400 are called senior masters or are referred to by their FIDE titles.

Material refers to captured chessmen. If you have captured more points than your opponent, then you are material ahead.

Middlegame is the phase between the opening and the endgame. While specific openings and endings may be memorized, middlegames feature the creation of long-term strategies and calculations of tactics. In Figure gloss.2, a student records a checkmate that occurred in the middlegame.

Figure gloss.2.
Checkmate in a middlegame position.

Moves in chess refer to either making a move (i.e., half of a move pair) for one side, or to the combined white and black move pair. Thus when a chess problem reads, "white to move" it is white's turn. But when the problem states, "white checkmates in three moves" that means three white moves (with the required black moves also played), that is, a white move and black move; a second white move and black move, and a third white move completing the mate.

Opening refers to the first 10 or so moves of a chess game, during which time players develop most or all of their pieces. The opening is followed by the middlegame, which is followed by the endgame. In Figure gloss.3, a student considers her next move in an opening.

Pairing is the assignment of opponents and colors (white or black) in a tournament.

Pandolfini, Bruce, is a USCF master, prolific chess writer, and sought-after chess teacher. His instruction of elementary student Josh Waitzkin, who later attained the IM title, was featured in the 1988 book and the 1993 film *Searching for Bobby Fischer.*

Passed pawn is a pawn that has no enemy pawn opposing it on its own file or on an adjacent file. Thus a passed pawn is a likely candidate for promotion.

Pawns (P) are the smallest units on the chessboard. They move forward, but capture diagonally. A pawn may move one or two squares on its initial move, and when it reaches its eighth rank it is promoted. *See also* promotion; en passant.

Figure gloss.3.
Playing an opening.

Perpetual check is when one side may check the other side's king continually and the checked side is unable to stop the checks. The game is either a draw by agreement or as a case of the threefold repetition of position rule. *See also* draw.

Pieces are not pawns, but rather include kings, queens, rooks, bishops, and knights.

Pinned chessmen are lower-value pawns or pieces that shield a higher-value piece from an enemy queen, rook, or bishop. The lower-value chessman is pinned if, when it moves, the higher-value piece could be captured by the enemy. For example, an enemy bishop could pin a knight to its queen. If the knight moved off the bishop's diagonal, the enemy bishop could take the queen. The previous example is a relative pin, because the knight could legally move. An absolute pin occurs when the higher-value piece is the king. In that case the pinned piece cannot legally move, as moving exposes the king to check.

Points are a guide for the fair exchange of pieces. That is, just as one wouldn't want to trade $9 for $3, one would likewise usually refuse to trade a Q (9 points) for a N (3 points). Points can also refer to a player's score in a tournament, that is, "He has one point" means that he either won one game or drew two games. Points can also refer to chess rating, as in "Alexey Root's current USCF rating is 2002, which is 260 points lower than her peak rating of 2262."

Position is the arrangement of the pieces and pawns on the board.

Post mortem is conducted after a chess game is completed. The participants in the game discuss their moves, sometimes joined by interested observers.

Problem is a chess position (usually represented on a diagram) in which there is a specified solution. For example, a problem might state "White to move and mate in three." The person studying the problem would either set up the diagrammed position on a chess board and figure out the three moves, or solve the problem mentally.

Promotion is when a pawn reaches its eighth rank and is converted to a N, B, R, or Q. One usually queens a pawn, as a queen is the piece worth the most points. *See also* under-promotion.

Queen (Q) is worth about nine pawns, according to most sources. On any given move, she can choose to move like a rook or like a bishop.

Queenside is the half of the board that includes the d-, c-, b-, and a-files.

Ranks are the horizontal rows of squares on a board. There are eight ranks, labeled 1, 2, 3, 4, 5, 6, 7, and 8 in algebraic notation.

Rating is a number assigned to a player based on his performance against other rated players. USCF ratings range from the low 100s to around 2800, with a mean of 1500.

Redactive instruction "is a method of teaching that allows multi-move problems to be simplified by editing them backward from the solution" (Pandolfini, 1995, p. 206).

Removing the guard means to capture or drive away the pawn or piece defending another pawn or piece.

Resigns is to accept a loss before being checkmated. When resigning, tip over your king or say "I resign" to your opponent.

Rook (R) is a chess piece that moves horizontally and vertically, as many squares as are not blocked by its own pieces. It can capture an enemy piece or pawn that is in its path. The rook is usually said to be worth five pawns. *See also* castling.

Sacrifice means to deliberately give up material to achieve an advantage such as a checkmating prospect against the enemy king or the promotion of a pawn.

Score sheet contains the notation for a chess game, as written by one of that game's participants.

Set of chessmen is the combined collection of 16 pawns, four rooks, four knights, four bishops, two queens, and two kings. Half of the set are black pieces and pawns; half are white.

Skewers and pins are tactics directed toward two enemy pieces on the same line (diagonal, rank, or file). In a skewer, the high-value piece is first along the line of attack. When it moves off the line, the newly exposed piece of lesser value can be captured.

Stalemate is when a king is not in check but there are no legal moves for his side. It is scored as a draw.

Staunton chess sets are required at FIDE tournaments. Designed by Nathaniel Cook in 1835, the set is named after the great English player Howard Staunton (Eade, 2005, p. 337).

Tactics are moves that force short-term sequences to win material or another advantage. Some common tactics are pins and forks.

Touch-move rule states that if players touch a particular pawn or piece then they have to move it. If they touch an opponent's pawn or piece, then they must capture it. Once they remove their hand from a chessman, the move is completed and cannot be changed. If a legal move is impossible with the touched pawn or piece, another move must be selected. If a chessman simply needs to be straightened, say "I adjust" (or the French term *J'adoube*) and then replace the pawn or piece on its square without penalty.

Tournaments are chess contests among more than two players. Tournaments have rules about time controls (*see* clocks), pairings, and behavior (one can't get chess advice during games).

Tournament directors (TDs) run tournaments according to the rules of chess, either the USCF rules or the FIDE rules.

Trade is to exchange your pawn or piece for your opponent's.

Trap is "a move whose natural reply results in a disadvantage to the replying player" (Eade, 2005, p. 338).

Under-promotion is "the promotion of a pawn to a piece other than a queen" (Eade, 2005, p. 339).

United States Chess Federation (USCF), main Web site http://www.uschess.org; sales Web site http://www.uscfsales.com/. The USCF is the official governing body for chess in the United States. It also runs the USCF rating system, which ranks member players, and produces a monthly magazine, *Chess Life.*

Variations are alternatives to the moves that were actually played in the game under analysis. Also, "Any sequence of moves united by a logical, purposeful idea, either played in a game or proposed by an analyst. Also a specific opening line, such as the Dragon Variation of the Sicilian Defense" (Pandolfini, 1995, p. 261).

Wall chart for a tournament tracks the round by round scores of each player in cumulative fashion. By the end of round two, for example, a wall chart will likely have players showing the following scores: **2** (2 wins), **1.5** (one win and one draw), **1** (two draws, or one win and one loss), **.5** (one draw and one loss), or **0** (two losses).

Wins in chess occur when one player checkmates the other player, or when that player's opponent resigns or loses on time (*see* clock). A win is scored as one point for the winning player on the tournament wall chart.

World Champions (World Championships) are currently decided in tournaments administered by FIDE. The overall world championship was first determined by a chess match (two-player contest) in 1886; the first Women's World Champion was crowned in 1927. GM Judit Polgar competed for the overall World Championship in 2005 and in 2007; her oldest sister GM Susan Polgar held the Women's World Championship title from 1996 to 1999. GM Garry Kasparov held the title of World Champion through FIDE from 1985 to 1993 and through the Professional Chess Association (a rival organization to FIDE) from 1993 to 2000.

References

Chart of National Standards

Figure R.1 quotes national standards in the first column. Each standard has its own table. If available, grade-level expectations are listed in column two. The third column lists the activities in this book which thoroughly address the standard. Each activity meets one math or science standard, except for *Know More, Move More,* where the teacher selects the academic content. *Practice Producing Polygons, Chess Players' Stats,* and *Map My School on a Board* meet two standards each.

If applicable, tables are separated by grade level served. Science text is quoted from National Research Council (1996); math text is quoted from National Council of Teachers of Mathematics (2000).

Science as Inquiry Content Standard A	As a result of activities in grades K–4, all students should develop	Activities that meet the Standard
	Abilities necessary to do scientific inquiry Understanding about scientific inquiry	Chapter 2: 20 Questions, Criteria Challenge, The Good Bishop; Chapter 4: How to Castle, Move Order Mystery

Science as Inquiry Content Standard A	As a result of activities in grades 5–8, all students should develop	Activities that meet the Standard
	Abilities necessary to do scientific inquiry Understanding about scientific inquiry	Chapter 2: Pawn Game 3-on-3, Black Box; Computers and Checkmates; Stalemate Surprise

Earth and Space Science Content Standard D	As a result of their activities in grades K–4, all students should develop an understanding of	Activity that meets the Standard
	Properties of earth materials	Chapter 2: Physical Properties of Pieces

Earth and Space Science Content Standard D	As a result of their activities in grades K–4, all students should develop an understanding of	Activity that meets the Standard
	Earth in the solar system	Chapter 2: Chess Models

Earth and Space Science Content Standard D	As a result of their activities in grades 5–8, all students should develop an understanding of	Activity that meets the Standard
	Properties of earth materials	Chapter 2: To e.p. or not to e.p.

History and Nature of Science Content Standard G	As a result of activities in grades K–4, all students should develop an understanding of	Activity that meets the Standard
	Science as a human endeavor	Chapter 4: Openings around the World

Number and Operations Standard Instructional programs from prekindergarten through grade 12 should enable all students to—	Expectations In grades 6–8 all students should—	Activities that meet the Standard
Understand numbers, ways of representing numbers, relationships among numbers, and number systems	work flexibly with fractions, decimals, and percents to solve problems	Chapter 3: Pawns, Pieces, Proportions, and Probability; Chess Players' Stats
Understand numbers, ways of representing numbers, relationships among numbers, and number systems	develop an understanding of large numbers and recognize and appropriately use exponential, scientific, and calculator notation	Chapter 4: The King's Chessboard
Compute fluently and make reasonable estimates	develop and use strategies to estimate computations involving fractions and decimals in situations relevant to students' experience	Chapter 3: Chess Players' Stats

Geometry Standard Instructional programs from prekindergarten through grade 12 should enable all students to—	Expectations In grades 3–5 all students should—	Activities that meet the Standard
Analyze characteristics and properties of two- and three-dimensional geometric shapes and develop mathematical arguments about geometric relationships	identify, compare, and analyze attributes of two- and three-dimensional shapes and develop vocabulary to describe the attributes	Chapter 3: Practice Producing Polygons; chapter 4: Learning Chess Pieces
Specify locations and describe spatial relationships using coordinate geometry and other representational systems	make and use coordinate systems to specify locations and to describe paths	Chapter 3: Practice Producing Polygons
Use visualization, spatial reasoning, and geometric modeling to solve problems	identify and draw a two-dimensional representation of a three-dimensional object	Chapter 3: Covering the Board: Rooks
Use visualization, spatial reasoning, and geometric modeling to solve problems	recognize geometric ideas and relationships and apply them to other disciplines and to problems that arise in the classroom or in everyday life	Chapter 4: Map My School on a Board; The Knights Can't Wait

Geometry Standard Instructional programs from prekindergarten through grade 12 should enable all students to—	Expectations In grades 6–8 all students should—	Activities that meet the Standard
Apply transformations and use symmetry to analyze mathematical situations	describe sizes, positions, and orientations of shapes under informal transformations such as flips, turns, slides, and scaling	Chapter 3: Transforming Figures
Use visualization, spatial reasoning, and geometric modeling to solve problems	use visual tools such as networks to represent and solve problems	Chapter 3: Covering the Board: Kings; Eight Queens; Mazes and Monsters

Measurement Standard Instructional programs from prekindergarten through grade 12 should enable all students to—	Expectations In grades 3–5 all students should—	Activity that meets the Standard
Apply appropriate techniques, tools, and formulas to determine measurements	develop, understand, and use formulas to find the area of rectangles and related triangles and parallelograms	Chapter 3: Perimeter and Surface Area of the Board

Data Analysis and Probability Standard Instructional programs from prekindergarten through grade 12 should enable all students to—	Expectations In grades 6–8 all students should—	Activities that meet the Standard
Understand and apply basic concepts of probability	compute probabilities for simple compound events, using such methods as organized lists, tree diagrams, and area models	Chapter 3: Pick a Pocketful of Pieces

Problem Solving Standard	Instructional programs from prekindergarten through grade 12 should enable all students to—	Activity that meets the Standard
	apply and adapt a variety of appropriate strategies to solve problems	Chapter 3: Working Backward

Communication Standard	Instructional programs from prekindergarten through grade 12 should enable all students to—	Activity that meets the Standard
	communicate their mathematical thinking coherently and clearly to peers, teachers, and others	Chapter 4: Kasparov versus the World

Representation Standard	Instructional programs from prekindergarten through grade 12 should enable all students to—	Activity that meets the Standard
	create and use representations to organize, record, and communicate mathematical ideas	Chapter 3: Balancing Chess Equations

Connections Standard	Instructional programs from prekindergarten through grade 12 should enable all students to—	Activity that meets the Standard
	recognize and apply mathematics in contexts outside of mathematics	Chapter 4: Map My School on a Board

Figure R.1.
National Standards in Science and Math.

From *Science, Math, Checkmate: 32 Chess Activities for Inquiry and Problem Solving* by Alexey W. Root. Westport, CT: Teacher Ideas Press. Copyright © 2008.

References

Magazine articles can be obtained by contacting the magazine. Most of the books are available from online booksellers. When a particular book is not readily available, I've included ordering information in that reference's entry.

Barber, D. (2003). *A guide to scholastic chess.* Retrieved October 13, 2007, from http://www.amchesseq.com/gutoscch.html.

Basman, M. (2001). *Chess for kids.* New York: Dorling Kindersley.

Birch, D. (1993). *The king's chessboard.* New York: Puffin Pied Piper. (Original work published 1988.)

Eade, J. (2005). *Chess for dummies* (2nd ed.). New York: Hungry Minds.

Fine, R. (1941). *Basic chess endings.* New York: David McKay.

Gobet, F. (1999). The father of chess psychology. *New in Chess, 8,* 84–91.

Gomi, T. (1993). *Coco can't wait.* New York: Macmillan/McGraw-Hill. (This big book was created by the publisher by enlarging the selection as it appears in the student anthology *Goodness Gracious Me!* Level 3 of Macmillan/McGraw-Hill Reading/Language Arts.)

Khmelnitsky, I., Khodarkovsky, M., & Zadorozny, M. (2006). *Teaching chess step by step.* Montville, NJ: Kasparov Chess Foundation. (Schools may order a complimentary set of three books [1-Teacher's Manual, 2-Exercises Manual, and 3-Activities] by following the instructions at http://www.kasparovchessfoundation.org/.)

King, D. (2000). *Chess: From first moves to checkmate.* Boston: Kingfisher.

MacEnulty, D. (2006). Tips and tricks for teaching total beginners. In T. Redman (Ed.), *Chess and education: Selected essays from the Koltanowski conference* (pp. 113–122). Dallas: Chess Program at the University of Texas at Dallas. (Order for $28.00 [non-Texas residents, price includes $3 shipping] or $30.06 [Texas residents, price includes $3 shipping and $2.06 state tax]; direct orders and inquiries to Tim Redman at redman@utdallas.edu.)

McNeil, J. D. (2006). *Contemporary curriculum in thought and action* (6th ed.). New York: John Wiley & Sons.

National Council of Teachers of Mathematics. (2000). *Principles and standards for school mathematics.* Reston, VA: Author.

National Research Council (U.S.). (1996). *National science education standards: Observe, interact, change, learn.* Washington, DC: National Academy Press.

Nottingham, T., Wade, B., & Lawrence, A. (1998). *Winning chess piece by piece.* New York: Sterling.

Pandolfini, B. (1991). *Chessercizes.* New York: Simon & Schuster.

Pandolfini, B. (1993). *Beginning chess.* New York: Simon & Schuster.

Pandolfini, B. (1995). *Chess thinking.* New York: Fireside.

Pelts, R., & Alburt, L. (1992). *Comprehensive chess course* (3rd ed., Vols. 1–2). New York: Chess Information and Research Center.

Polgar, S. (2006). *Chess training program for teachers.* New York: Susan Polgar Foundation. (E-mail PolgarFoundation@aol.com to request a free copy of the PDF document [62 pages].)

Polya, G. (1957). *How to solve it: A new aspect of mathematical method* (2nd ed.). New Jersey: Princeton University Press.

Purves, A. C. (1975). The thought fox and curriculum building. In J. Schaffarzick & D. H. Hampson (Eds.), *Strategies for curriculum development* (pp. 105–122). Berkeley, CA: McCutchan.

Root, A. W. (2006). *Children and chess: A guide for educators.* Westport, CT: Teacher Ideas Press.

Root, A. W. (2006, October). The paperboy and the chess master. *Chess Life,* 27.

Seirawan, Y. (1998). *Winning chess openings.* Seattle, WA: Microsoft Press.

Shenk, D. (2006). *The immortal game: A history of chess, or how 32 carved pieces on a board illuminated our understanding of war, art, science, and the human brain.* New York: Doubleday.

Smith, P., & Daniel, C. (1975). *The chicken book.* Boston: Little, Brown.

United States Chess Federation. (2004). *Let's play chess.* Retrieved December 30, 2006, from http://www.uschess.org/beginners/letsplay.pdf.

United States Chess Federation & Kurzdorfer, P. (2003). *The everything chess basics book.* Avon, MA: Adams Media.

Watkins, J. J. (2004). *Across the board: The mathematics of chessboard problems.* Princeton, NJ: Princeton University Press.

Wolff, P. (2005). *The complete idiot's guide to chess* (3rd ed.). New York: Alpha Books.

Yalom, M. (2004). *Birth of the chess queen: A history.* New York: HarperCollins.

Index

About the Author

DR. ALEXEY W. ROOT has a PhD in education from the University of California, Los Angeles (UCLA). Her work history includes full-time public high school teaching (social studies and English), and substitute teaching at all grade levels. Root has been a tournament chess player since she was nine years old. Her most notable chess accomplishment was winning the U.S. Women's championship in 1989. Since 1999, Root has been a senior lecturer at the University of Texas at Dallas (UTD). She has taught UTD education classes, tutored prospective teachers for certification exams, and supervised student teachers. Root's current assignment for UTD is to teach education courses that explore the uses of chess in classrooms. Her courses are available worldwide via the UT TeleCampus online platform. Her *Children and Chess: A Guide for Educators* was published by Teacher Ideas Press in 2006. Root also teaches chess at her children's schools and at summer chess camps. She lives in Denton, TX, with her husband, Doug, her children Clarissa and William, and two house rabbits. Her e-mail is alexey.root@gmail.com.

CPSIA information can be obtained
at www.ICGtesting.com
Printed in the USA
FFOW04n1452060118
44370597-44084FF